Additional praise for
The Road to Self

"To know John Goodman is to love him. He is seen by those who know him as one of the kindest and most generous beings on the planet. In this book he openly explores his personal challenges in the hope that lessons learned will help others to chart a course for a brighter, more successful future. There are times in all our lives, when the forces around us seem too overwhelming—whether it be financial circumstances or health. John offers a simple prescription for those moments—that there is an incredible human capacity to both heal thyself and to intuitively know the right path, if you just choose to listen. Though not adhering to traditional religious precepts, John offers a guide to success and happiness that focuses heavily on love and faith. Qualities that are within the reach of each and every one of us."

—Former U.S. Senator Norm Coleman

"John Goodman's book, *The Road to Self*, is an amazing journey on the lessons of life with incredible analogies to life in every chapter. What John shares in great undertones is that everyone must work at giving back. He is one of the most generous and philanthropic people I have ever met and I have learned many life lessons from him, most importantly to live in the moment and trust in the universe. This is a must read for anyone."

—Steven Schussler, Bestselling Author
It's A Jungle In There and Creator of Rainforest Cafe, T-Rex, Yak & Yeti and The BOATHOUSE at Walt Disney World Resort® in Lake Buena Vista, Florida

"Few, who have attained the measure of success that John Goodman has, share their own bumpy road of life that we all experience. That makes *The Road to Self* particularly important. Those who read it will get new energy and understanding of life ahead."

—Former U.S. Senator Rudy Boschwitz

"A marvelous peek into the life of a Minnesota grown boy and CEO, John B. Goodman whom I've known for 26 years. He strips away the myths and falsehoods of that title and reveals himself the charismatic man who has more depth, dimension and humanity than anyone I've ever known. This is an unexpectedly fresh and immensely moving portrait of the man, John B. Goodman.

This is the kind of book you pick up intending to read only a couple of pages, and half a day later you find you've consumed the whole thing."

—Carole Hemingway, Astrologer and Author

"John Goodman's *The Road to Self* is an easy read with so many wonderful messages, lessons, and introspections."

—Sue Zelickson, Food Columnist, Community Volunteer, Founder of Women Who Really Cook

"John Goodman has been a loyal friend of mine for close to 25 years. I met him in 1990 when I joined First Bank System in Minnesota. John, his father and their companies were long time customers of FBS. Their businesses are very successful and one of the premier, privately held operations in Minnesota.

John is honest, loyal, generous, thoughtful and kind as was his Father Sid, first-class in every respect. He helps everyone without them asking. The world is a better place because of him. I am proud to call him a great friend and feel lucky to know him."

—John "Jack" Grundhofer, Chairman Emeritus US Bank

Also by John B. Goodman

Moments Matter, Everyday Inspiration from a Soulful CEO

The Road to Self

The Road to Self

REFLECTIONS FROM A SOULFUL CEO

JOHN B. GOODMAN

JBG
CHASKA, MN

Published by
John B. Goodman
c/o The Goodman Group
1107 Hazeltine Boulevard, Suite 200
Chaska, MN 55318

Publisher's Cataloging-in-Publication Data
Goodman, John B.

   The road to self : reflections from a soulful CEO / John B.
   Goodman. – Chaska, MN : John B. Goodman, 2015.

   p. ; cm.

   ISBN13: 978-0-9980001-0-7 (hardcover)
          978-0-9980001-8-3 (softcover)

   Businessmen—Conduct of life. 2. Success. 3. Self-realization.
   I. Title.

   HF5386.G67 2015
   650.1—dc23   2015939406

Project coordination by Jenkins Group, Inc.,
www.BookPublishing.com

Creative Director, Yvonne Fetig Roehler

Cover design by Black Retail

Interior design by Brooke Camfield

Printed in the United States of America
19   18   17   16   15 • 5   4   3   2   1

1920–2013

*To my father Sidney,
a true shining star.*

Contents

Foreword

*T*he *Road to Self* is an exciting, insightful book filled with practical, spiritual nuggets throughout. John has hit the ball out of the park with his delightful, reader-friendly prose that is sure to help countless business and non-business people alike.

Vulnerability, honesty, and transparency set *The Road to Self* apart. It opens the reader to experience these concepts through unique and moving examples applicable to many aspects of every-day life.

We have known John Goodman for over twenty-five years and share with great certainty that this man lives what he writes and walks his talk. It takes a tremendous amount of courage to share the up-and-down challenges that he has experienced in the particularly guarded world of business. John shares stories of his previous loneliness and how in the past he has used "busy-ness" to hide out from his own feelings. It is rare to find such a suc-cessful businessman who has developed the profound ability to communicate with deep conviction and passion about the power of love and the intrapersonal challenges of fear.

John is crystal clear about his belief that the same spiritual principles in one's life can be applied both personally as well as professionally. And, in fact, the only way to be a real success in life is to integrate both by having harmony and integrity in all that we think, say, and do. He does so by leading us on a journey to become the trusted friend of our truest Self.

Today, there is a great hunger and thirst for another way of looking at the world where anger, blame, and stress play such important, negative roles. John creates literary road signs that make it much easier to navigate in the world that our physical eyes thought they saw.

As John continues to share the inner learnings of his heart, we discover that all of us have the capacity of courage to choose our own inner peace and love that has always been there. He shows us that we can choose to act more consciously in our lives, to teach and demonstrate only love. Then the fearful world we once thought was real starts to disappear and love becomes the reality we experience.

Gerald G. Jampolsky, M.D. and

Diane Cirincione, PhD

Co-Founders—Attitudinal Healing International

Preface

Change can be challenging. In 1990, I made the decision to leave everything I knew to find true happiness. As managing partner of The Goodman Group (formerly the Sage Company), I was growing and expanding the company my father Sidney started in 1965. I joined the company in 1970 and, although I was successful in business, I was not successful in my personal life. I found myself alone and struggling in my relationships. I was searching for greater happiness but did not know what path to take. So, I went on a quest, a road trip to California to find some answers and garner the peace I had been seeking. While traveling over 2,500 miles, I documented my experiences and thoughts about business and my personal life.

My ultimate hope is that by sharing the lessons of my journey, it may help others discover their answers. I believe if I can help just one person, this book will have been a worthwhile endeavor.

Acknowledgments

I am very grateful to all the people who've helped me learn in this classroom called "Life." This book wouldn't have been possible without you. Also, if I were to name everyone, we'd be here for a while. So thank you for your dedication, guidance, and care. You know who you are.

CHAPTER

I

Learn from Life

At a young age, I was told business is easy, but relationships are hard. That belief became ingrained. As a result, I have been quite successful financially and in business. However, in terms of relationships, I often found myself in an emotional desert. I was fortunate to get married at thirty-one, but the marriage lasted only four years. I had no idea how to prepare for what the world calls commitment.

Some people in my life have accused me of being unfeeling and insensitive. I didn't want to be that way. It's just that I wasn't equipped with the proper emotional tools or training. When it came to putting a business deal together, constructing buildings, or buying apartment complexes, I was quite adept. In fact, although

1

we started in residential real estate, I soon became inspired by the nature of the deal and what demographics we could serve or what needs could be met. Building retirement homes and healthcare communities was a way for me to express caring. However, when it came to knowing what I needed within or how to communicate my feelings, I was often at a loss. Today, I realize that business life and personal life are one and the same and I can show compassion and gratitude in all my relationships.

Learning about emotions often starts at home. The rule around our house was that children should be seen and not heard. We were told, "You make a better door than a window." It wasn't right for a man or a boy to show emotions. A boy always had to be strong and independent, and it wasn't okay for me to ask for help or for what I needed. When I did, others always seemed too busy tending to their own needs. This is no reflection on my family. The situation encouraged me to learn lessons, grow in my spirit and soul, and help others with wisdom and insight into why we face difficulties in life. But, I'm getting ahead of myself.

Let's go back to the beginning. When I was very young, maybe three years old, we lived on Glenhurst Avenue in Minneapolis in a modest home. I remember our neighbor, the tree in front of our house, and crawling out of my crib trying to get upstairs to my parents' room. I seem very joyful in my memories. As a child, I was running and active, always looking to learn. Then we moved to a new, more expensive house on Basswood Road. My father was a struggling beer salesman, and he worked very hard to support the family. I don't remember much about those first years in our new home. I do remember having my own room. I also see a child sitting in his bedroom hunched over and terrified.

With a new home came changes. We now had a succession of housekeepers, and through later analysis, I realized that I suffered sexual abuse at the hands of one of them. Fortunately, that house-keeper did not stay for long. I think that was when I reached some conclusions as to my vulnerability and how I related to women. I didn't discover this until many years later, after I was divorced and underwent intensive counseling. Reflecting on my early childhood, I realize that feeling powerless gave me a better understanding of what people endure in life and helped me evolve into a more com-passionate human being.

Ultimately, we are not victims in life. Everything we experi-ence lets us learn lessons that help us evolve. Knowing this, we can remove ourselves from apparent dramas. We can learn through pain, sorrow, and suffering. I hope, that as the years progress, I can learn life's lessons without the intense suffering they often seem to entail. We all have had past hurts and conditioning. We must be resilient and heal if we want our lives to be better.

CHAPTER

2

Trust the Universe

Dysfunction can continue for generations. At the age of forty-one, I was holding on to negative belief systems because they were familiar to me. However, there comes a time to let go and rewrite the script. Sometimes that isn't easy because hanging on to the familiar seems safer than venturing out into the unknown. It had taken me years to get to this stage. I'd cling tenaciously to what I thought was right and the way I thought things should be.

My road trip to California allowed me to reconnect to nature and the universe. It also showed me that the universe will intercede and put you where you need to be when you need to be there. You must choose whether you want to hang on and fight change, or learn and let go. Once you get out of your own way and let your ego take a backseat to what your heart says is right, you will experience tremendous growth and learning.

Time and again the universe has reminded me to live in the moment and trust that I'm where I'm meant to be. There are no accidents. In fact, on the road to California, I drove into a small town and didn't read the signs properly, so I wasn't quite sure which way to go. About three blocks beyond my missed turn, I pulled onto a side street and eventually parked. Moments later, somebody drove up behind me, got out of his truck, and told me that my muffler was hanging. Fortunately, I was only a block away from a gas station. The muffler was dangling by one hook and, had I continued on, it would have broken off or been severely damaged. Five minutes and five dollars later, I was back on the road again. I marveled at how easily that situation was fixed. The universe works in amazing ways and if we learn to flow with it, everything gets taken care of in its own time.

Even in business, situations occur and we need to let them flow, trusting in the ultimate timing of events. For example, in 2013, our nonprofit organization was to partner with a local hospital to build a senior housing project next to our office. Because the project was a partnership of two nonprofit entities, we were getting financing through the sale of tax-exempt bonds. After our groundbreaking, we were selling the last of our long-term bonds. At the time, Ben Bernanke, head of the Federal Reserve, talked about cutting back the bond repurchase program, and as a result, no one wanted our long-term bonds and the project was put on hold.

When we finally arranged to get another source of financing, the construction costs went up by 25 percent making the project unviable. Years ago, I would've worried about the outcome. Now, I realize the universe was protecting us, and we're now exploring new opportunities with new joint venture partners. I trust if the project is to get done, it will and if not, it is not ready at this time or may never be.

CHAPTER

3

Let Go, Let Business Flow

When I reflect back, I realize the universe has constantly guided me in business. For example, our company was trying to build a nursing home in Florida, and a neighbor took us to court claiming that the Certificate of Need transfer was unlawful. My first impulse was to rant and rave, believing that this was a malicious suit. However, as I quieted myself and entered my stillness, I realized the universe was saying that it wasn't time to build this community and that when the true time arrives, the universe will help.

In the past, I would bulldoze past these signs, saying, "Boy, I'm going to do this no matter what," and then I'd learn my lesson. When those gut feelings tell you what you're doing isn't appropriate, but your ego gets in the way and you push forward, you have to live with the results. There is no shame, no criticism, and no "I told you so." The results are there so you can learn and perhaps not have to repeat such a long and arduous process.

Using a more trusting philosophy does not mean passivity or an inability to function. It means the ability to "let go and let God," knowing that there is a higher power. Now, your "God" can be a religious God, or it can be nature or the universe, or however you envision your higher power. The more you try to force events, battle the natural flow, and try to control things, the further out of control things get. We can't necessarily change events, but we can certainly change how we respond to them.

In the late 1970s, our company acquired a 638-unit apartment project on thirty-three acres in Largo, Florida, called Imperial Palms Apartments. We bought that property from a company called U.S. Homes. Adjacent to the complex was a forty-five-acre tract of land, and I constantly looked at that land and imagined what could be done with it. U.S. Homes had tried to develop a project on it, pouring foundations in the early 1970s. Unfortunately, when the real estate market became difficult, the company abandoned its plans and let the land sit, foundations and all.

Meanwhile, our company surveyed the residents at the apartments and discovered that their average age was seventy-four. We realized we could build assisted living with retirement housing next door for when they couldn't take care of themselves. So, in 1981, I made a deal with U.S. Homes to take over the master lease on this tract. We drew up plans, and I tried to obtain bond financing in 1983 and 1984. I was turned down both times by 4–3 votes, so the project ground to a halt.

In the late 1980s, I had a meeting with U.S. Homes in their Minneapolis office. Their property was right off a freeway but nestled among trees and overlooking a pond. I told the representative, "This building would make a great office for somebody." I gave the idea no more thought and returned to our St. Louis Park office where we'd been for over nineteen years. About three months later, U.S. Homes called and said they wanted to sell the office in Minneapolis and wondered if I knew anyone who might be interested. I said, "No, but I will keep my eyes and ears open."

A few weeks later, I had a strange dream about occupying that office building. I kept thinking about it and one day told U.S. Homes that our company would buy the building. After the purchase, we sat on it for about a year and a half during which I got calls from people wanting to rent or buy it. However, I felt strongly that we should keep it. At that time, our Minneapolis offices were connected to a hospital. Sure enough, one day the hospital offered to buy the entire building!

We weren't able to build the Florida project because we had been turned down for bond financing. However, when the hospital bought our Minneapolis office, we traded our interest in it for the Florida project and moved into the building we had bought from U.S. Homes. It seemed like everything quickly fell into place, but in reality, it took over ten years.

Originally, I had thought we were stuck with forty-five acres in Florida that couldn't be developed because we couldn't find financing. Actually, it became one of the most positive developments in our company's history. I realized that when we got turned down for financing, it wasn't time to build the project in Florida, and the universe, in its divine way, interceded to keep me from getting into financial difficulties. By waiting, we were able to finance the project with very little debt and see what everyone else in the community had succeeded or failed at. We built something that was architecturally right because we had developed other projects and knew what to do and what not to do. Today that project has over 1,700 residents and employs 800-plus people in a unique intergenerational community that includes residential apartments, assisted living, healthcare, memory care, and more. We also donated adjacent land to the city of Largo for a community center.

Earlier in my life, I experienced another opportunity to trust the universe. In 1966, my father wanted to purchase a 201-unit apartment project in Las Vegas, which had been foreclosed on by the US Department of Housing and Urban Development. Having no money, but being resourceful, he got thirty partners to invest $10,000 each, and we operated it for about twenty years.

Then The Mirage Hotel was built. Our property happened to be on the corner of its site, and we started getting inquiries about selling. Half the partners preferred a real estate exchange to a sale, hoping to avoid the capital gains tax. Unfortunately, this is more complicated and requires the trade property to be identified within a six-month period. That job fell to me. I knew I had to find the right project for the right amount of money in the right part of the country. I thought this would be quite difficult, but even though I faced tight time constraints, I decided to sit back and see what would happen.

Less than ten days after entering the exchange period, we got a call from a company in Lima, Ohio regarding a nursing home it owned in Safety Harbor, Florida. The home was licensed and ready to open, but the company had a conflict of interest and wanted to sell. I toured the nursing home and, a few days later, made a deal. By trusting the universe, our trade property was identified within two weeks and we were headed to closing. The partnership was happy with the property, and it fit well in our portfolio.

I couldn't have created these situations. They involved synchronicity, fate, or whatever word you might choose, but they resulted from allowing the process to flow. If I had thought I had to find that trade property at a certain time, in a certain location, or that it had to be a certain size, I would have limited the possibilities. I would never have thought to look for nursing facilities where we own quite a few apartments. By not limiting our company or myself, I let the universe flow and bring what was appropriate for us at that time.

CHAPTER

4

Stop Comparing

I've often found myself asking why I don't have something, or why this person is liked, or why I appear not to be. Whatever the reasons for our existence, it's important that we avoid comparing ourselves to others.

When I was fifteen, there was a very respected social group that everyone hoped to join. However, it required an invitation. The first year I was eligible, I wasn't asked. I thought, *what is wrong with me?* The next year I was passed over again, and I doubted myself even more. Finally, I was invited to join, but it was bittersweet.

Not being asked the first two years stuck inside me, gnawing away. I assumed many things were wrong with me and still were wrong. Finally, in college, I asked a friend why I hadn't been invited sooner. He laughed and said he'd been jealous of me and stopped my nomination. He thought it was too easy for me to get girls and people liked me. I was shocked! I was thinking I wasn't good enough while he was thinking he was less than me. We had both wasted valuable time and energy.

Since that epiphany, I have come to understand that regretting every heartache is a waste of time. If we chose this existence, we came here to learn our own unique lessons. It would be more appropriate to say: "I chose this for a reason." Or, "There is wisdom to be gained from this experience." Maybe I'm not consciously aware of it at this moment. Maybe it's buried in my subconscious mind where most of our information is stored.

It's important to release attachment to all that we aren't, all that we don't have, and all that we wish we could be. We should recognize our divinity and the beauty of our existence. This is a lesson I'm still applying to my life. I keep thinking about the things I haven't done or about the things that I should be doing, and I rarely acknowledge what I've done with my life or admit that it's okay just to exist, knowing that whatever I need will come to me when I need it. Instead, I have spent a lot of time trying to control things and figure out my next move.

We all know people who have changed jobs or been fired because of cutbacks or family transitions. I tell people in our company that if they aren't happy they should leave because they aren't doing themselves, the organization, or any of the people they come in contact with any good. I think some of them stay because they think making a change wouldn't be financially safe and wouldn't allow them the success they seek.

Sooner or later, though, the universe intervenes and prods people to make a change. The natural state is to be happy in what you are doing. The majority of us aren't, though. If you're not, you need support to find what motivates you, what makes life exciting and worth living. A person who loves what he is doing connects to others because he feels this passion from the depths of his heart and conveys that. A salesperson, for example, who believes in the product has a much better chance of success than a person who is just mouthing words and doesn't have that belief.

If I could wish only one thing in life for all people, it would be happiness in what they do every day. People who are content with their lives always impress me. They could be bricklayers, musicians, accountants, teachers, or work at any other occupation, but they're happy with their situations. They live in the moment and appreciate where they are rather than constantly trying to change their circumstances. If they realize that they're not satisfied, they can make a change and do something else, trusting the universe will support them.

Ultimately, life is about feeling, not just about doing and thinking. We must balance body, mind, spirit, and emotion, never stressing one at the expense of any of the others. If we're constantly in a state of discontent, it wears on us physically and emotionally. Sooner or later, we will have to get to the root of it and change our situation so it becomes more satisfying and supportive.

CHAPTER

5

Embrace Change

On my way to California, I drove by the remnants of a forest fire. It was interesting to see all the charred land and wood. Yet there were little baby trees sprouting up, standing tall, and reaching toward the sky. Devastation brings change, but out of that change comes a new entity that is striving to grow, flourish, and take its place. This process is akin to what happens in our lives as things are taken away or as people leave through death or the ending of relationships. Through this perceived devastation comes a glimmer of hope. Growth begins and new life is nurtured by its surroundings, becoming a little stronger, a little taller, and a little surer of itself each day. Ultimately, the tree is strong.

We also must learn to bend with the wind, as trees do. If we're rigid in our beliefs and attitudes, we will break and perish. I tried to make my trip safe by telling myself I would just drive to California, spend a few days, and then return. When it hit me that I was leaving my home and everything familiar, it was damn frightening. I had none of the old support that kept me comfortable. In my moment of out-and-out terror, I knew the universe was testing my connectedness to the spiritual being inside me and that I should learn to trust. I don't know if you have to leave old surroundings to have this process work for you. I think you can succeed at any moment, in any place, when you're willing to let go of the past, the desire for control, and the notion that everything must be done the way you have always done it.

Some people can easily adapt to change, and some are much more reluctant. My sun sign is Taurus, and I have four other planets in Taurus too. People born under the Taurus sign are known to be stubborn, so I have had difficulty in letting go and giving up old patterns. Those patterns may not have been safe, may not have served me well, and may not have contributed to my happiness, but they were familiar.

Most of us gravitate toward the familiar, and people don't usually say, "This is the way I have done it, but you should take a totally different path and find out what's right for you." Instead we're given little bits of wisdom that coincide with our family members' belief systems. We learn from them and, therefore, tend to experience life the way our parents did. In examining dysfunctional families, psychologists first look at the grandparents because their family system is passed on to our parents and ultimately to us. If we're not able to break the chain and heal the wounds, the problems get passed down to our children.

We must figure out how to let go of patterns that aren't helping us to live in a joyful way. This doesn't mean giving up everything we've learned. We must identify what's productive for us as individuals and replace what's not productive with ideas and situations that are more conducive to leading a happy life.

If some people feel right, then we can allow them to remain in our lives. If they don't, we may need to change how we perceive them, or set appropriate boundaries for how we want to be treated. This can bring our relationships to a new level of awareness and understanding that makes us feel joyful to have certain people in our lives. At a certain point, however, some people may just have to go.

In letting go of old beliefs, we allow a new set of beliefs to enter. This is valuable in terms of our careers. For example, in deciding to make a career change, we face fears about economic survival and wonder what will happen if we end up worse off or can't find a job and can't support the family. Those concerns are valid, but in talking to people who have left jobs over the years, they all said the change was the best thing that happened to them.

One of our employees owned a company prior to working for us. He thought of his job with us as a temporary step and always had one foot out the door. One day, he said he was going to change the way he viewed his job; he was going to jump in with both feet. Now, instead of worrying about what he would do next, he wanted to be totally committed to what he was doing, for however long it lasted. Though the job didn't change, he was willing to let go of his old perception of it. Since then, he's become a much more productive employee who seems more settled, present, and joyful.

Before a trapeze artist can grab the second trapeze, he or she must let go of the first. At the brief point between the two, indecision and fear come to the surface, but without letting go of one there's no possibility of obtaining the other. In life, as we allow one door to close, another will open. But many times we may miss out on valuable opportunities because we want the certainty that the second door will open before we are willing to close the first.

CHAPTER

6

Look in the Mirror

One day I looked in the mirror and noticed a pimple on my nose. I kept finding fault with myself, wondering when will I be good enough? When will I accept myself with the damage that's been done and with the errors that I've made? When can I just look in the mirror and say, "You're okay, you're where you're supposed to be, and you're doing what you're supposed to be doing?" Of course, we can't look back at yesterday and say we should've done something differently because that's already happened and it can't be different. It's exactly what it's supposed to be. But if we had it to do all over again, would we do things differently? Maybe if the opportunity presented itself, we would decide to take a different turn in the road to achieve a different outcome.

In the past, I often looked back on my marriage and wished I'd been better able to handle the commitment, to be a more loving husband. Now I understand that the loss of my marriage helped me learn how to be committed and how to act in an intimate relationship. In addition, I think it was an opportunity to awaken self-love. I will always treasure that experience. I believe the universe is forgiving. I believe we all have another chance, whether it's a new relationship, friendship, or another job. The universe continually gives us opportunities. It's our responsibility to learn from our mistakes and challenges so that when we face a similar situation, we can choose a better path.

We also should examine what binds us to situations that work or don't work. Many of us are still attached to what we learned in childhood. These attachments are often subconscious. I have an attachment to finding someone similar to my mother, and I've been working on letting that go. I know that if I'm to attract someone I want to be with for the rest of my life and who wants to be with me, I have to stop looking for that person and work on myself. I must make myself a healthier human being and let go of preconceived ideas about what a woman should be.

Everything we face in life is a mirror, so we need to look at what people and situations reflect concerning our behavior and thought processes. Do you know people who leave one relationship and quickly enter another just like it? Though the names change, the circumstances and the outcomes remain pretty much the same. One of my friends has had multiple marriages, and he keeps attracting the same type of woman. The only difference is the woman's name and perhaps her hair color. He continues to put himself in situations where he is dominated and controlled.

This implies no criticism of the people you meet because we're all simply mirrors for each other. Another person can be a reflection of where you're at in a given point in life. If you leave your home or office feeling angry, notice what you attract. People will approach you with scowls on their faces. They will be short-tempered and show anger in their movements, speech, and facial expressions. If you're joyful, light, and free, you'll attract friendly, kind, and supportive people.

I returned from a trip to meet with nursing home administrators. This was the first time in years that I'd felt so calm and peaceful and we got a lot of work accomplished with little pressure. Staff members told me they felt the same way. I realized that my energy had changed and now I was attracting a different energy.

Children are wonderful reflectors of others. If you are short-tempered and cross with them, it's amazing how cross they will be. If your tone of voice exudes peace and calm, you will sense those qualities in the child. Tone of voice is very important because most people can tell what you're saying not by the words, but by your inflection.

I once took a neuro-linguistic programming class taught by Dr. Dave Dobson, a hypnotherapist. Our assignment was to go to a shopping center, pick an individual, study that person, and then approach and mirror them. We were told to mirror their breathing, facial expressions, and posture. The outcome was amazing. When we approached our subjects, they were instantly at ease with us. In fact, one person came up to me and said, "I know I know you," and he wouldn't accept the fact that we hadn't met before. I was mirroring back to him his own reflection, breathing rate, facial expression, and stance, and he was quite comfortable with that because it was a reflection of who he was.

If you're attempting to build rapport with people in business, for example, meet them where they are and accept them. This will create a connection between you. If they're in a space that is trying for you, break the pattern. See what happens when somebody is angry and you smile or offer a kind word. The change in them will be automatic. If somebody is joyful and you also feel that way, rapport is instantly built.

Ultimately, if you want certain qualities in a relationship, I truly believe that you must first exhibit those qualities in yourself. We must let go; work on our issues; and get beyond the blame, shame, and guilt aspects in our relationships. We must look within ourselves to see how we caused a relationship to happen the way it did. As we heal and come to a greater level of understanding, we may realize that what we attract is the reflection of the person we are inside.

CHAPTER

7

Choose No Limits

In years gone by, people thought they'd work at their jobs and when the time came for them to retire, all would be happy and well. Unfortunately, we're finding that isn't the case. Given our long life spans, retirement is not a valid concept for many people. Some people in their seventies are functioning well, and some choose not to stay at the same job for forty or fifty years. Given our longevity and many choices, maybe we're supposed to experiment and go through multiple stages in life. Instead of staying at one job forever, maybe we should stay in a job only if we feel productive and happy, believe that we are contributing, and continue to enjoy the give-and-take that is so essential to life. When that feeling dissipates, society should make it easy and safe for people to move on to work that rekindles their joy and their sense of being alive.

There are no limits in life except those we choose to put upon ourselves. I chose one limit that was particularly interesting. When I was thirteen, I was preparing for my Bar Mitzvah. The rabbi told me that given the quality of my voice, I would be better off saying the words rather than singing them. Ever since then, I've been reluctant to sing. Part of me wants to sing, to change the tone in which I relate to others.

Tonal quality is important, and an expressive style comes naturally to every child. Yet, as we age, we increasingly speak in monotone. We become dead to feelings, and this is reflected in the intonations and the melodies of our everyday speech. It's a joy to hear how children express excitement with their voices. Their speech is congruent with their manner. Listening to myself, I realized that I had adopted a more monotone style. The inflection was gone, and the excitement no longer seemed to be there, although I know deep inside that it never left me. All of us are born with it, but as time passes, society finds a way to mold it, limit it, and box it in.

Life should be melodious. It should be joyful. I think our schools are creating people who react from memory rather than from the heart. They seem to put more emphasis on achievement than on learning. Why can't we express ourselves? When my son started kindergarten, his teacher told his mom and me that she thought his hearing should be tested. When I asked why she thought this was so, she said he spoke too loudly when he entered the classroom. We had him tested, but we knew his hearing was fine. We knew he was happy to be at school, wanted to participate, and felt confident when he walked into a room. Why should he be quiet? Why should he limit himself? Why should he be seen and not heard? These are the questions we should ask for every child *and* for every adult.

As a society, we can accomplish much if we encourage our children to be who they are, to feel who they are. We can let them make mistakes and grow. We can nurture them like flowers and give them love, support, and understanding. If even one of us does that with one child, it will make a tremendous difference in that child's life when he or she becomes an adult.

CHAPTER

8

Accept Yourself

Many people, including me, are high achievers. We have goals we want to accomplish, status that we want to obtain. With upscale homes and the newest model cars, from the outside we appear to have beautiful living situations, yet on the inside we long for connectedness to spirit. Despite what we have and what we are trying to obtain, our satisfaction is fleeting. Are we finding joy in the external rather than the internal? Do we realize it has to come from within?

Increasingly, people are searching for internal peace, happiness, and joy. I believe we will find these things, each in our own way. Every situation in life or business—becoming an ally or facing a hurdle that we must overcome—offers us a glimmer of hope and an opportunity to experience and to learn. How we live and how we feel is up to us.

For most of our lives, we're taught to trust other sources, our schools, our churches, and our partners, but we aren't taught to trust ourselves or our own innate abilities. There's always somebody who knows more, knows better, and can tell us what to do and how to do it. We need to know that we're all part of God's creation and that part of God is in each one of us, and it's important to connect with it. If we can learn to trust ourselves and our connectedness to spirit, we can go within and find the answers that we need to face life's trials and tribulations.

We should accept ourselves as we are—knowing that we are beautiful and that we already possess all we need to be within creation. That lesson is a difficult one for high achievers to learn, because we've always been taught that we need to do rather than to be. In school, we were never graded on participation. We were always graded on how we did on exams, and showing up wasn't enough. We were constantly pitted against one another in competition. We were taught that we always have to do more, be more, and get more in life, and along the way we can lose sight of our true essence.

We can find everything we need within us. We must accept and enjoy that part of ourselves instead of buying into what everyone else says we are based on our ranking in school or because someone complimented or criticized us. We must come home to ourselves, accept ourselves as being enough, and get in touch with the God-like energy in each of us.

CHAPTER
9

Live in the Moment

I've always looked toward the future with a desire to accomplish something of importance whether it's writing a great American novel or doing some deed that benefits mankind and helps the environment. Companies such as Cargill and Honeywell have done a tremendous amount through socially responsible philanthropy like introducing inner-city youth to the corporate environment. I have a wish that my company, in time, will be known for leaving the world a better place. That is one of my dreams.

Unfortunately, if we're always pursuing the elusive dream, we might never see or realize what we're accomplishing now. So our achievements may slip unnoticed into the past without recognition, acceptance, or appreciation. If I'm always looking forward to creating something or doing something, then I never take pleasure in what I'm doing at the moment, and I might never see the value of what I've done.

I realized that if I believed what I was telling myself, I should put it to a test. I must ask whether I trust that I am where I have to be, contributing what I need to be contributing, at that moment, in my own way. We must step outside of ourselves, and if we help just one person, that's significant. If we were taught that more is better, then it's time to reprogram. It's time to say to ourselves, "You know, it's okay. Everything will come in due time and in due order." Why not just accept where we are? Why not relish it? Why not cherish the lessons that we're learning and forgive ourselves and others? You have to love yourself before you can accept yourself and vice versa.

Constantly looking forward, we lose sight of where we are in the moment. The future is but a dream and the past is just a memory, so if we are not living in the present, we spend our lives either in front of or behind ourselves. If we're content to live in the moment, knowing that God's divinity or the inner spirit is working toward its purpose and that all is right with the world, then what happened yesterday or what might happen tomorrow should not be important. Tomorrow should be influenced by how we feel and how we think at this moment.

How many times do you find yourself saying, "If only I had done this or that" or "tomorrow I'll do it better"? Should haves, would haves, and could haves all involve judgment. Author Arnold M. Patent cautions that it does no good to sit in judgment of others or ourselves because life is an ever-changing experience and nothing is stationary.

CHAPTER

10

Listen

Shortly after my divorce, my ex-wife told me, "Your son feels you don't listen to him. He feels you're not there for him." My first reaction was to get defensive and say, "What do you mean? I spend a lot of time with him." Yet, when I thought about it, I realized she was right. When I was with my son, I was looking over his shoulder, concentrating on something else. I spent time on the telephone, saying, "Just a minute, son. I'll be with you in just a minute." I took phone calls during dinnertime, a time we said that we would commit to one another, a time when we would talk, with no TV. I always allowed the phone to interrupt whatever bonds we were establishing. I finally decided that there would be no more phone calls or interruptions so I could truly be with him. I soon found that when I was there and really listening to what he had to say, our bond grew. Our love for one another flourished because of how we spent our time together. I think this has relevancy for all relationships.

There was another time when I realized I too needed to be heard. One day, I was meeting some friends at a restaurant and I was eager to discuss a question about fatherhood. Interestingly and somewhat surprisingly, after I raised the topic, I was suddenly under fire. I got six different opinions. One person said, "You're screwed up, and until you get yourself straightened out, you are not going to be any good to your son." Another told me, "You should go home and be with your son a lot more than you are, because you travel too much."

They said that I had brought my son into this world and that I had a tremendous responsibility to take care of him. One person said I didn't appropriately discipline him.

As the conversation continued, my friends told me what they thought I was feeling and offered advice about what I should do. Finally, an astute member of the group said, "John, how are you feeling?" I replied that I was feeling very defensive and felt I had to justify my parenting and explain what I was doing correctly. My friends said that I shouldn't feel defensive and that I should know that they cared about me and loved me. They said that they were simply offering their opinions about the best course of action. I realized that this moment was like so many in my life. Somebody might ask me what I was feeling, I would reply, and the person would say it was inappropriate, that I shouldn't feel that way.

I've come to understand we must learn to accept other people's feelings and resist the urge to judge them too harshly. I asked what I thought was a simple question, but it sparked opinions, observations, and the grading of my parenting abilities. This is similar to arguments that people might have in relationships. A discussion of a single issue can spread like wildfire to include all kinds of situations and past events. Soon a person is being judged for his past, present, and even future and all sorts of outside components are being introduced. Before long, people don't even know why they are arguing, because the discussion has nothing to do with the opening issue. That's what I saw happening that morning.

It also is interesting how others always seem to have a prescription for someone else's life. I've found that some people use projection and diversion so they don't have to deal with their own issues. It's easy for people to point a finger at what you did rather than take responsibility for what they are doing.

I learned a lot from this discussion. I examined my ability to parent and what I was doing that was appropriate and what areas perhaps I could improve. I decided that I was going to be even more involved in my son's life. I wasn't going to get down on myself and feel guilty. This doesn't mean I am abdicating responsibility. I am looking at my role and my responsibilities and doing what I feel I can do best, and I will not punish myself because I might have done things differently.

I also realized, in order to develop good listening skills, we have to be quiet and avoid thinking about what the person is going to say next. We also have to listen to ourselves and be focused in the moment. When we allow others to express themselves we learn that it's okay to show feelings. We don't have to criticize, argue, or fight back. We have to learn that it's all right to listen without giving an opinion, without making a judgment, without contributing something or adding to what another person is saying. Being in the moment, without thinking of the future or dwelling on the past, is a wonderful gift that we can give others and ourselves.

CHAPTER

II

Balance Your Diet, Balance Your Life

They say intuition is God talking to us through our thoughts. It's also possible that God talks to us through our bodies. Unfortunately, we don't always listen to what's being expressed. We crave what isn't necessarily good for us or we go without rest or without taking time to nurture our temples, to dwell in the body. The body, the spirit, the mind, and the emotions all work in concert, so if we're not taking care of the body physically, we certainly aren't taking care of ourselves emotionally or spiritually.

Too many times we are consumed with guilt, with shame, with how we're supposed to look or be. We prefer these things to acceptance, to nurturing and supporting our own being, to recognizing that the outside is a mere shell. The inside is more important, and nurturing the inside takes the proper diet, rest, and exercise.

37

Stubbornness has driven me for many years to go without proper nutrition or sleep and to avoid taking time to stop and listen to my body. As a result, I'd become short-tempered and unkind to others and myself. Though we all wish we could be different and change overnight, life doesn't work that way. We must stop what we are doing to change the cycle. As the saying goes, "If we always do what we've always done, we always get what we've always gotten."

While in California, I visited the Pritikin Center for a week to learn about eating and nutrition. Sometimes I've had problems with my diet and with my kidneys, liver, and spleen. At other times, I've been quite healthy and felt fine. The difference is like night and day.

Before going to Pritikin, I made sure I ate all the unhealthy things that I liked. In fact, two hours before I was supposed to be there, I was at a birthday party for a friend, eating as much cake and ice cream as I could get into my mouth. The next day, the Pritikin staff did a blood test and found my cholesterol was close to 190, which is on the high end of the optimal range. I decided to give up sugars, fried foods, and other fare that wasn't in the Pritikin plan to see what the outcome would be and how I would feel.

The Pritikin method is based on moderation. You have three and a half ounces of meat, fish, or poultry a day and you don't eat fried or salted foods or foods cooked with oils. You can eat all the vegetables, fruits, and grains that you desire, and you are encouraged to eat more regularly. For example, after breakfast you may have vegetables or fruit at mid-morning. You may also eat vegetables or fruit in the afternoon, after lunch before dinner. By eating this way, I no longer experienced weight fluctuations, which has improved the way I feel and increased my energy.

Most of the people at Pritikin have had some type of illness, are in their later years, or have to go based on a doctor's recommendation rather than out of choice. It would be great if people could learn this type of program without having it forced on them by illness or as a last resort. Individuals and businesses could help implement this type of nutritional counseling in our school systems. That would go a long way toward helping children prevent some of the major illnesses experienced by previous generations.

The more you honor your soul's temple, the body, the clearer you become, the more energy you have, and the more you become centered and able to live in the moment. We need to reexamine our philosophy of doing whatever we want and assuming that someone will help us if we get sick or that a cure will be found for the disease we suffer. We must stop treating our bodies poorly and expecting someone to heal us later. Let's look at the source. An alcoholic may stop drinking but still exhibit all the tendencies of an alcoholic because he hasn't gotten to the root of the problem. That's why introspective programs are wonderful in helping alcoholics and their families. They get to the root of the problem rather than just trying to stop symptoms.

A little over a month after I finished the program, my cholesterol level fell from 190 to 148. In addition, some of my other blood factors became more normal. I also felt a tremendous increase in energy and felt more stable and centered; I didn't seem to be flying off the handle. In the past when I would get angry, I would immediately reach for a candy bar or something else containing sugar. But sweets only escalated my feeling of panic and shortness of temper. I found that my system couldn't handle sugar. Dropping it made a great difference in the way I feel, the way I respond, and in my weight and my outlook.

CHAPTER

12

Rewrite the Script

I used to smoke a pack of cigarettes a day. Every time I quit, I gained weight. How many times have we been told that if we quit smoking, we will suddenly eat more and gain a lot of weight? So what happens? We quit smoking and we gain weight. That happens because we're told it will happen. However, in my experience, this doesn't have to be the case.

In the late 1980s I decided to quit smoking on the same day author and motivational speaker Tony Robbins was in Minneapolis for a firewalk. In this event, people walk over a bed of coals in their bare feet. This may sound heroic, but participants are well trained, and anyone from seven to ninety years old can do this.

In this particular instance, we practiced over and over in our minds what we would say ("cool moss") and pictured ourselves walking across the bed of coals ("cool moss"). Actually accomplishing the feat was anticlimactic because we had done it so many times in our minds. We also had been asked to write down any fears and be prepared to throw them in the fire. I wrote that I was afraid that I couldn't quit smoking and that ultimately I would get sick and die. At that moment I knew that I was truly ready to give up cigarettes. When I walked across those coals despite my fear, I finally realized that my fear of being unable to quit smoking and of dying was just something I had created and if I could overcome one fear I could certainly overcome another. I quit that day and did not gain weight.

Anybody can do this. It's a matter of believing you can and then rewriting the script. Why should you believe someone who says if you do one thing another thing will happen? Is everything we are told gospel? Because something has happened once, does it always have to happen again? I have always been amazed at how relatives sometimes die at a similar age from a similar disease, and I have often wondered whether genetics are at work or whether people believe what they're told about their prospects for longevity. If my grandfather and my father had heart attacks or strokes, am I doomed to the same thing? Should I give up necessary nutrition because I am fated to suffer as they did?

We can rewrite the script at any time, and all it takes is a change in our belief system. In changing that belief system, our behaviors, attitudes, and actions change also. Not knowing where we're headed may not be so bad as long as we know what we're leaving behind. Maybe we picture our bodies as being healthy; maybe we go within and we see white light around our organs and the blood flowing through them rapidly and clearly.

I don't intend to get into a debate over the benefits of medicine versus the benefits of spiritual wellness. I know that nothing is black and white and that genetic issues are involved. However, there have been numerous examples of people who've changed their physical being by changing their attitude. Many practicing Buddhists will tell you they can affect their heart rates on different sides of their bodies through meditation and visualization. If we believe that we can think ourselves into illness, then why can't we think ourselves into wellness?

I've mentioned people who've had heart attacks and were changed by that experience. The health of our bodies depends on our willingness to bend and to change. Are we willing to move forward and to let go of negative belief systems and negative patterns? If not, our bodies will talk back to us to the point where we will be forced to change. It's amazing how the universe turns up the volume. If we don't get the message the first time, it will reappear in a different form and at a higher volume. How many times have you experienced an unusual event and only a day or two later suffered a cold, stomachache, or some other illness?

The only way some people can express their feelings is through illness. They equate bad feelings with feeling bad, and therefore their bodies have to go through an emotional cleansing, perhaps by a cold or the flu. If people were allowed alternative ways to express emotions such as anger or frustration, maybe they wouldn't resort to feeling sick. As children, when we weren't feeling well, we could always get the attention we were longing for to make our hurt feelings go away. How many times do we, as adults, resort to feeling bad so we can feel good again?

One time, I was suffering from a herniated disc in my back, the result of a waterskiing injury. I had been told numerous times that I should have an operation and that the disc was so herniated that it was forever gone. An MRI showed there was no question that it was out of place, but I believed it would heal in time. My goal was to look at an X-ray and see everything back in place. Just because I'd been told that was not possible, why should I believe it? Since the waterskiing injury, I've herniated my disc three times. I've also healed it three times, the first time taking six months and the last time taking only two weeks.

We have been given tremendous talents, and yet we've not learned how to use them. They are part of our divinity. We must go within and discover the skills that every one of us possesses. If we trust ourselves, we can develop these gifts.

In January 2012, I was hospitalized because of pneumonia. The medical community told me that my left anterior descending artery (LAD) was 100 percent shut down. They told me I had previously suffered a heart attack. However, in doing their tests, they found they did not need to put stints in or perform bypass surgery because somehow I had created a new set of collateral arteries.

The issue revolves entirely around energy, and if we learn how to deal with energy and let it flow through us, it might help dissipate our illness. Our psyche might change, and we could nurture ourselves in a positive, loving way through nutrition and our thoughts. Maybe we will find ways that are not as painful as the old ones.

CHAPTER
13

Recognize Your Oneness

Years ago, a respected hospital chain in Minneapolis was interested in doing a joint-venture senior housing project on one of their campuses. They were somewhat familiar with us because they knew some of our partners. They visited our office, and we sat and talked about the project. At first I found myself responding to what was important in business: how the project would do financially and how it would help the community. I was saying what I perceived to be all the right words.

Then an interesting thing happened. About halfway through the meeting, my son walked in after school, and the whole tone changed. It became much more real. I recounted the story of how we found our office building and said I felt if a deal is meant to be, it would fall into place. I also spoke about a Native American artist named Joe Geshick (1943–2009), who had done quite a bit of artwork for our offices. His philosophy was that life is a spiritual adventure, and he used his artwork to promote an artist colony in the Southwest that emphasizes spiritual awakening and awareness.

The president of the development company said, "Part of my family is Native American, and I have a relative who paints pictures that are in my office and whose qualities are very spiritual, warm, tender, and compassionate." At that moment, it was no longer two companies coming together to do business and make a lot of money. Instead, it was two people who could identify with human evolution and with the warmth and tenderness of being human. Our common interest in children and the human spirit connected us. We understood not only our own strengths and frailties but also the difficult times of Native Americans. We expressed appreciation for the great gifts and talents that they possess.

Throughout time, rituals have been important to every culture. Many have been lost. We have taken people and segregated them. We put Native Americans on reservations. We put seniors in nursing homes. We put children in front of television sets. It's time to reestablish rituals and connectedness. Religion and spirituality play an important part in our traditions and so does family.

However, increasing numbers of people are drifting away from religion, and more and more families are breaking apart because of economic pressure or the loss of loved ones. As time goes on, our responsibilities will change. No longer will we have the luxury of only loving family members. We will need to love and support one another. Community must be established. Segmentation by race and religion will have to end out of necessity so people can help one another to survive.

Growing up Jewish, I certainly saw a divergence of opinion about Jesus and his function. What I am discussing here is more universal and more spiritual because it affects all of us, whether we are white, black, Jewish, Catholic, or Protestant. A God-like spirit resides in each of us, and we realize our connectedness by widening our minds, stilling our voices, and connecting with nature.

As the years pass, I think family ties in all countries will lessen. I met a Japanese legislator at our Florida project and he said Japanese families are having difficulty staying together. It was once the responsibility of the eldest son to care for senior family members, but that has changed because families no longer live in the same towns, more family members must work out of economic necessity, and divorce has become more common. In many cases, there are no family members present and the elderly have no one to help them.

Change may come through force or out of choice, but it will happen. We've seen this for centuries as societies have come and gone. In many instances, people failed to bend or to flow, staying strong in their dogma and feeling that their way was the only way. We can start at any point and affect change, but we have to trust and allow what evolves to evolve naturally, the way it should be, and with dignity and grace.

CHAPTER

14

Choose Social Responsibility

On my way to California, I passed by Bear Lake in Idaho, a magnificent setting except for one thing: the shoreline was eroding tremendously. What used to be water had become a sandy flat, and the marina was up for sale. The situation is hard to fathom. When you look at the beauty and the splendor of the area, you wonder why this is happening and why the weather patterns are changing.

This change really hit home for me when I was in Australia, and the astronaut Pinky Nelson spoke to our business group about space and the universe. He said he had been up in space many times but there had been a five- or seven-year stretch between two of those trips. When he finally went up again, he saw a tremendous change in the earth's shores, beach areas, and river deltas. The enormous erosion was clear from space. He also said the burning of the rain forest was quite visible.

It is our responsibility to ensure that our beautiful environment is maintained for generations to come. Groups concerned with environmental responsibility in business are becoming a new force. They believe that business can be an agent for social change. If business leaders allow a more benevolent philosophy to permeate their companies, it will affect employees, the people they deal with, and ultimately the community. From there, national and international forces will be affected. I believe very strongly in what these groups are doing. One such association is the Social Venture Network, and another is the World Business Academy. These organizations believe that you can do well by doing good. Businesses needn't give up the profit motive, but with a new attitude we can all win.

In the late 1970s and in the 1980s, companies incurred tremendous amounts of debt to finance acquisitions. These deals might have been fine for the few people who held the stock, which soared in price, but they certainly didn't add anything of value for employees. In fact, in many cases, when one company purchased another, employees were let go immediately or sometime thereafter. These deals forced increases in prices and/or decreased the quality of the products being offered.

Social responsibility has become more of a concern out of necessity as we progress into the twenty-first century. Perhaps our definition of value in a company can be expanded to include not only financial results but also social results. In keeping with the Japanese philosophy, company leaders will see that there are no shortcuts to success and that they must determine their company's long-term effects on an industry. They must reevaluate their corporate role within society and decide how to build a firm base of employees and loyal, satisfied customers.

Companies are no longer places where people go to spend eight, nine, or ten hours a day before returning home. Our community in Largo, Florida, houses seniors, single-parent families, medical facilities, and a learning center for children. While workers are busy in the workplace, children and seniors interact and help support, teach, and learn from one another. Everybody wins in this situation. Our vision is to create communities that offer training in empowerment, team building, wellness education, and efforts to balance body, mind, spirit and emotion. Wellness programs and esteem-building courses could be used for children and seniors as well. We believe this will help reduce the tremendous costs for employee health plans and improve employee satisfaction.

This sort of corporate setting could be created in existing communities if the real estate is not available for a standalone complex. These new intergenerational communities would help people support one another. Because of greater constraints on public funding, corporations must play more of a role, and because of changing demographics in the coming years, it will be increasingly important that we regenerate a sense of community in existing neighborhoods as well as in new areas. Seniors can be helped in performing daily functions, and they in turn can help those who need guidance, such as children whose parents are off making a living. By taking these steps, we can truly become connected and be respectful of the earth and its people.

CHAPTER
15

Live Fearlessly

While traveling, I found a useful metaphor for the concept of living in the moment and being mindful. I was faced with driving curve after curve, and they were very sharp, steep, and angled. Unless I concentrated on every curve as it appeared, I could have driven right off the road. If I was thinking about the curve around the bend or the one I had just negotiated, I couldn't focus on what was happening at that moment. In life, we face curves in our daily living. If we learn to concentrate on what is taking place at the moment and try to negotiate our present situation, we can come through almost any experience safely.

The sunrise, a day spent in the heat, and the sunset tell me something about how we live our lives. We're born with the hope of a new day and then we grow under the sun. We're nurtured and pass slowly from one point in the sky to the other, moving from childhood to our teen years and into midlife, then into later life. The finality of the day's end can be equated to the finality of life's last moment, but there is always another dawn. This is also true for each of us. Another dawn awaits us and another adventure, only in a different form or energy field. If we believe that we've chosen this life and we've chosen other lives prior to this, then we know that this is but one of many lives that we'll live throughout time. And, if that's the case, why should we live in fear of death?

I used to think death was a drama. When I was seven years old, I saw my parents crying profusely. I was scared and wanted to know what had happened. I didn't know what to do, and neither did my parents. When I asked them what was wrong, in tears myself because of their panic, they told me that my maternal grandmother had passed away. That singular moment had a profound effect on my thinking about dying and death. Ever since that day, I looked at death as something to be feared and have thought it was waiting around the corner for me. Because my uncles died early of heart attacks, I thought I would pass away of a heart ailment at a young age. But who taught us that death should be feared?

My company manages and develops a number of senior housing communities, and one of our goals is to reassess how we view aging and death. If we look at it as a transition, like the sunrise and the sunset, we will view death as just another experience. We will be here for as long as it takes to learn whatever it is we need to learn or to do whatever it is we need to do. Then we'll choose to go on to the next experience. I've seen a lot of people make the transition from this plane to the next, and many seem to have an inner knowledge of when it's time to leave. My mother Georgine was fifty-eight when she passed away from breast cancer. Unbeknownst to us, in the days before she went for hyperthermia treatment, she had told friends that she knew she was not going to come out of the operation. Sure enough, while she was on the table undergoing treatment, her heart stopped and she passed away.

My friend Zola was eighty-six and had spent a lot of time in the hospital. He was very ill, but he rallied and came home. He looked good, he sounded good, but he told me he wasn't happy. He didn't like being cooped up in the house unable to take a walk every day as he used to do. On the Sunday before his passing, he was jovial and feeling well, but somehow we both knew that it was time. He'd had enough and he had done enough, and it was time for him to make that transition. On Monday night, he went to sleep, got up in the middle of the night, and experienced his heart attack. It was sudden and he went without any pain. I think he finally decided to let go and move on to the other side.

Another friend, Sam, who had been sick for many years, experienced a long hospital stay and was at one point pronounced dead. He told an interesting story. For the minute-plus that he had been "dead," he had seen a light and felt at peace with himself. The next thing he knew they were banging on his chest, and when he looked up and saw a beautiful woman he thought perhaps he had, in fact, died and gone to heaven. He soon found out he was very much alive. After a year of being in and out of the hospital, he was released and on his way home. He told his wife that he was tired and that he didn't know if he wanted to continue. As he got out of the car and was walking to his house, he stepped off the sidewalk and onto the grass, lay down, and had a massive heart attack.

I believe we have a choice in our passing. Many of us think we don't, and so we believe we have to continue the struggle. More frequently, though, I've seen people give in to that subconscious urge when it's time to move on. A feeling of peace, a sense of lightness seems to come over them as their souls make the transition to the next plane.

Jim, another wonderful human being, worked as a high school track coach and was highly regarded in his profession. He was diagnosed with cancer in his late twenties. Doctors told him he didn't have long to live, and the news brought a lot of strain and hardship to the family. While in the hospital he met a wonderful nurse whom he later married and subsequently had a set of twins. They are the sweetest, most wonderful little girls you could ever meet.

Unfortunately, Jim died, but prior to his passing he called each one of the people with whom he was close into the hospital room and talked to them individually. He said that he was finished, that he had done all that he needed to do, and he said his good-byes. Peacefulness came over him as he made the transition to the next plane. Though he was young and his death was untimely, Jim's family knew that he'd done what he needed to do in this lifetime and touched all the people he needed to touch. When he left, he did so knowing that he'd accomplished his life's mission.

If we believe that people choose their coming and their going, then why not honor these choices? Why not celebrate, view death as a transition, and hope that one day our souls will connect again? Love is eternal and can never be taken away, lost, or terminated.

Recently, at one of our senior living communities in Florida, I told a group of eighty to ninety seniors that we would help them live healthier, more enjoyable lives and that when their time came to pass, we would hold a party for each person, invite friends, and share memories, photos, and videos of the person. We wanted to look at death not as an ending, but as a transition, and we would celebrate that transition as a rite of passage. Much to my surprise, almost everybody in the group applauded.

Once we give up our fear of death, ultimate loss of control, and nothingness, we can get on with living and know that we've chosen this experience. We will choose when to end this experience and to go on to the next one. Therefore we can live without fear. We can use whatever tools are available to help us spiritually, mentally, emotionally, and physically so that we can live in a healthier, more joyful state while we're here.

If we trust in our spirituality and believe that all is right with the universe, we can trust that we'll be supported in our transition or passing. We're never alone. We're always connected to that higher spiritual part of ourselves, and the unifying force throughout time has always been love. Sometimes we have a sense of a loved one who has passed on. We get a message, a feeling, or guidance, almost as if the person was looking over our shoulder. Spirits on the other side are there to help us. We always have that connectedness. Though a soul isn't tangible, it still survives and flourishes, and we remain connected.

On October 20, 2013, my son and I were blessed to be with my father when he took his last breath at the age of ninety-three. This was extraordinary! Over a period of months, we saw changes in his health. Toward the end of his life, we witnessed him going in and out of the here and now. He said things like "take me home; I want to go upstairs and see my family." He mentioned family members who had already passed. This experience made me rethink life and death. I realized that a person's form might change, but not their energy.

Almost five months after my dad's passing, still being some-what skeptical, I asked for a sign that he was still around me. Two days later, a young man came online looking for Dad and me. He was the son of a friend who had passed away years ago. Although we had only met him once when he was a young boy, out of the clear blue he tried to contact us. At that point I knew Dad had reconnected with this man's mother on the other side. This was the sign I needed.

CHAPTER

16

Heed Your Dreams

We have dreams for a reason. Pay attention to them and the feelings that arise through meditation. During those quiet times, those dreamlike states, messages come to us, and our guides are there to help support us. Next time you have a strong sense of something, pay attention to it. Play the hunch. Don't dismiss it as being insignificant or worthless. Know that you are guided and supported as you learn to listen to that inner voice. It's there for you whenever you want it, whenever you need it, whenever you call for it.

How many times have you talked to someone who's trying to figure out the solution to a problem? The person will keep thinking it over and over and then give up. Then in a flash, either in a dreamlike state or at a different moment in time, the answer will be there. The answers come when they are supposed to come and we need to trust this process.

The drive up Highway 1 from Santa Barbara to Carmel is beautiful, but I took the inside route, Highway 101, because it's quicker. Right before Highway 101 and Highway 1 split, I saw a palm tree in Pismo Beach with a sign that read Psychic Palm Reader. On my way back, I decided to stop. I knocked on the door of a seedy little shack and a woman answered. I asked her if she had time for a reading. She said she was busy but added, "You look troubled my friend; we should probably talk." I asked her how long I would have to wait and she said about forty-five minutes.

I left and thought *maybe I should, maybe I shouldn't*, but this seemed like a pretty interesting situation. Forty-five minutes passed, and I found myself back at this woman's doorstep. She said she could do one of three readings—cards for $25; palms for $35; or cards, palms, and psychic reading for $45. I wanted to get it all in, so I opted for the top-priced reading.

I was amazed at how accurate she was. She told me that I'd gone through a separation in my relationship and a divorce and that I was looking to relocate from another state and had moved to a residence in California, but would be there for only a short time before I would move to another residence. She also told me things about my marriage and my relationship with my ex-wife that she couldn't have known had she not been psychic. She said another relationship lay ahead with someone who would genuinely love me and that this was something I'd never had in my life. She said the relationship would be healthy and joyous.

I found myself accepting this. Sometimes when you're questioning your life, you get signals assuring you that you're on the right track. This would have been fine if that had been it, but now she said she could help me with my "vibes," because I needed to calm down and steady myself. She said she would be glad to help me do that for another $95.

I knew I had gotten my neck in a noose, but I was curious to see what this miraculous support would be, so I made the transaction. When we were done, she said that we would meditate and that every day at the same time she would meditate with me and help bring me calm and peace and everything else I needed in life. I thought this was fine and dandy, but she was starting to remind me of the women I used to meet when I was in the Coast Guard and had gone to bars. Girls would have you sit on the inside of the booth and they would say, "Do you want to buy me a drink?" And after three or four drinks, they would say, "Well, it's time to go," and they'd leave you sitting there alone.

I do believe in psychic and spiritual skills. If used properly, they can be very helpful. However, people are charlatans when they use their gifts to make others dependent or convince them that the power lies outside them. The first part of the reading was right on, but then I sensed that this individual's greed or ego took over. I questioned her motives when she professed an extreme concern for my wellbeing and began playing on my fears. However, I was free in my decision making and there were no hostages. I did this voluntarily, but in supporting one another, we need to be honest and let people know that all the answers are within. A skilled psychic, therapist, counselor, or coach reflects what people know inside already.

We all have an innate ability to listen to our inner voices. It takes practice and a quiet mind. It also takes forgiveness of self and an understanding and acceptance of shortcomings and frailties. Look at life as a classroom in which to learn. Sometimes you don't have the answers readily at hand, and sometimes you must discover what you still need to learn. We must let go of seeing everything in black and white, right and wrong, and focus on what we can learn from an experience.

CHAPTER
17

Live Your Story

On my way to California, the universe taught me another lesson. My good friend, astrologer Carole Hemingway, said it was a very fortunate time for me because I had a planetary aspect that takes place once every two years, and I would be lucky if I chose to gamble. I decided to stop in Reno and experiment. Whether I won or lost, I planned to stay detached and experience the results.

First I was down, then I was up, and when I finished the evening, I'd won some money. The next morning I took my winnings and went downstairs. It didn't take long to give all the money back. In the past, I would've been excited or melancholy over the outcome, whether it was gambling or business. I would've fought to win more or regain what I had lost. But I've learned there is great freedom in not being tied to what happens.

I'm thankful that I can let go more often and detach from the negative or the positive. Losing can get you down, but the excitement of winning is merely the other side of the coin. Detachment works well. You can appreciate things for what they are and not get hooked by the drama. Learn to say, "That's enough," then go on and let your story unfold.

I've traveled for work or vacation most of my life. I've had condominiums in Florida and Los Angeles, an apartment in Minneapolis, and a house in Minneapolis that I built. Yet no place has ever been home. A friend of a friend had some beautiful property in Santa Barbara. I don't know why, but I had a strong sense of place for that area and I thought I might choose to live there. I asked my friend to contact me if his friend ever decided to sell.

Time passed, and eventually, the man gave me a call. That night, I had a vivid dream about this land. It was high up and there was a marina on one side. To the west was water in a semicircle, and behind the point where I was standing were hills and scrub trees. The setting was clear. I talked with him again prior to visiting and asked about the land. Was there a marina on one side, the sun setting straight ahead, and was there water in a semicircle? He said yes!

I realized I was going to see this land for a reason. We hadn't discussed price or what exactly was available, and yet I was very trusting. I felt that if God told me this is where I needed to be at this stage of my life, I would create the home I never really had. I felt I was ready to put down roots, have a relationship and a family. I headed toward Santa Barbara with an inner knowledge that this land would be mine and that all the details about price and size would work themselves out.

I couldn't wait to see if my dreams accurately reflected what I would find in Santa Barbara. I also had seen an octagonal house overlooking the water and a sheepdog. There was also a family and a sense of joy. Maybe I would finally achieve my subconscious dreams that had been suppressed for so many years.

I traveled to the property, parked my car, and looked around. It was a magnificent view. I could see the marina down below, pretty much the whole 180-degree vista of water, and hills rising above. My host arrived and I commented on how lovely the land was. We headed down the road from the hill and toward a hiking trail. We discussed philosophies and some of our mutual friends, and after a few hours, the subject of the land came up. He told me that he and his parents had found the property and bought it. His parents had one house on it and he and his wife had the other. The land could be separated into four or five additional lots. He mentioned that his neighbor, a rock star, wanted to acquire one of them, but he wanted to know if I had an interest as well.

We hadn't gotten around to the price, and he asked me how high a number I thought it might be in my wildest, wildest dreams. I was somewhat reluctant to venture a guess. He'd been asking $1 million for one of the lots, and somebody had been interested but was turned down because he didn't like the house they were designing. I told him I couldn't afford that price, but if God wanted me to be on this land, we'd work out the details. If not, then we'd enjoy the hike and have a nice time together.

As we turned around, we passed through an Episcopal monastery sitting at the top of the property and then headed back down. We looked at the various parcels and I was drawn to a tract facing west behind the two houses. He told me he planned to build his dream house on this land; so, that section wasn't up for discussion. In addition, the lot didn't have a water permit. Santa Barbara was strict about issuing new water permits to control its growth.

I only had an interest in the one parcel and was willing to wait to see if I could get water to it. I trusted that one day, if I was supposed to build a house there, then I would, but I couldn't afford to pay $1 million. I told him that now wasn't a good time to negotiate on the land and that I'd wait and see. He mentioned the possibility that someday he and his wife could move, and if they did, he would see if he could work something out with me. For the time being, however, they wanted to hold this land for the family.

I spent the evening and part of the next morning with the couple. I had the sense that his wife thought I was an intruder because I wanted to buy their "dream home" parcel. As time passed, I felt a growing coldness between his wife and me. I realized that fate and destiny were working, and I saw visions of my house being built on the parcel that I wanted.

The next morning, driving back to Carmel, I experienced a lot of emotional chatter about my possible lifestyle change. Maybe now I could build a real home; I pretty much saw the house in my mind's eye. But, as I thought about building a home and a relationship with another human being, I questioned that lifestyle, wondering if I could adapt or whether I would like it. I found myself saying, "God, I need help with this." I realized I needed guidance letting go of past patterns, such as traveling all the time, and I needed support to reach an inner peace to accept a new lifestyle.

We will all experience times of hesitation or fear. I have mental images of living in a house high in the hills and being locked in there for days, weeks, and months at a time and going stir-crazy, and yet I know deep in my heart that's not likely to happen. Life would become more peaceful in this setting. One thing I especially liked about the land was the great hiking trail behind it, and I could envision spending time with my son and the rest of my family hiking and being with Mother Nature. I could also learn how to use the creative side of my being to write, paint, and sculpt.

As I've learned more and accepted more, I have come to believe that trusting God will put us where we need to be when we need to be there. If I'm to be someplace else, that is fine. If I'm to be on this land, that's fine. The key is not getting attached to the outcome.

As it turned out, I didn't buy that land in Santa Barbara. The process of letting go and trusting was a miracle in its own right. I've also come to realize that before I can have a physical space that feels like home, I need to find that home within.

CHAPTER

18

Confront Your Past

I have been very fortunate to work with a chiropractor who uses muscle testing for childhood issues so they can be brought to the surface and healed. Many people believe their thought processes were formulated in high school or in college. I have learned that a lot of our behaviors were developed in the first three, four, or five years of our existence. We tend to block them from our conscious minds so we don't remember them. We still respond to early childhood events in high school and college and even well into our thirties, forties, or fifties. We may do this for our entire lives.

Muscle testing and my work with the chiropractor led to some interesting conclusions. For one, I learned that lemongrass essence could help a person who feels rejected by their parents. By releasing the need to be nurtured by his parents, an adult can begin to nurture himself in loving and consistent ways. Very often the lemongrass personality will expand rejection from his parents into a general "love hurts" belief and manifest painful relationships throughout his life. Lemongrass essence will not only ease the pain but also change the person's attitude. One's perceptions and choice of who to love deeply will become more refined. As each of us learns to trust on an individual basis, we can reach out to love and embrace humanity.

The Goodman Group has established a company called Soulful Environments™ that makes use of essential oils as well as visual and auditory therapy to affect one's state of mind. One example of visual therapy is the exit doors at one of our memory care communities. People experiencing memory loss have the tendency to wander. When they see doors, they want to push them open, but these doors must be secured to keep residents safe. This can cause residents to become agitated. Our creative solution was to faux paint the doors to look like bookshelves filled with books, knick-knacks, and even a cat. Now people are calmer and no longer try to open the doors.

Through muscle testing, I realized that I had felt forgotten. I was responding to situations based on the emotions of a frightened four-year-old who didn't get appropriate bonding. Because of this, I would manifest relationships that ended in abandonment. For me to heal my inner child, I needed to bring those emotions to the surface, examine them, and reframe them.

Author John Bradshaw's work on the dysfunctional family is incredible and you may want to consider becoming familiar with it. He found that at least 90 percent of us come from dysfunctional families in one way or another. This dysfunction could involve physical, verbal, or sexual abuse. When people experience these situations in early childhood, they may continue to resonate to those frequencies until they are able to bring them to the forefront, look at them, and heal the emotional pain. To ensure that I bring into my space a healthy and sound relationship, I will continue to look at these issues until I can solve them. I will continue to do the work.

Unless you deal with the issues surrounding your emotions, you will inflict those issues on others. If you're on the receiving end, ask yourself what's really going on instead of moving into a defensive mode and fighting back. Take a step back and a deep breath, and focus on what else may be happening. What else is this person trying to say or do? Ask yourself what three things are not being verbalized. Emotional issues often involve something that happened a day, a week, a year, or even decades before or in childhood.

Apply the same principles to your own situation. Ask yourself whether you're responding to a problem in the current moment or to an underlying issue. Center yourself to come up with some answers. Perhaps you'll think about it at night when you're about to fall asleep. If you can come up with alternative explanations for what's taking place at any given moment, perhaps you can gain more insight into human nature and have more compassion for yourself and others.

CHAPTER
19

Find New Inspiration

I had been living in the same town, associating with the same people, and experiencing the same things for years. I had a set routine day in and day out. I lived three blocks from my office. When I was in town, I would get up, go to work, stay long hours at the office, return home, and socialize with friends by going out to dinner or visiting a club. My business was flourishing, but the other parts of my life weren't being nurtured or supported. I realized it was important to uproot myself from the known, the traditional, and the familiar patterns.

I wanted to act like a four-year-old, seeing the world as new, fresh, and bright. I wanted to expand my possibilities and capabilities, to experience life and gauge my experiences by how I felt. We must all get in touch with our feelings, clearly and concisely express them, and ask for what we want and need in life. Leaving gave me an opportunity to look at the creative side of my life instead of constantly working. I had time to take spiritual growth courses, creativity classes, and to learn how to balance my life so that I didn't favor any one area over another.

Each of us needs to find time to try something different. You don't have to move across the country. I needed a large undertaking to create a big impact, but you don't have to do that. You could start with regular meditation or spend time in nature, go for long walks, and be silent and contemplative. It's not necessary to turn your whole life upside down. In some cases, that may be what's required, but if your inner guide tells you otherwise, listen to it and ask what would help you be more reflective and what would bring you more peace of mind and inner strength. Try it even if it feels unfamiliar.

There are simple things we can try that can help us break the same old patterns. When you go to a bookstore, forget any preconceived idea of what you will buy or what subject matter you will peruse. Allow your intuition to help you discover the books you need to read. You will be drawn to subject matter that's relevant to you at that given moment. If you want to solve a problem or find an answer, you'll be amazed at how you're drawn to the book section that sheds light on your situation or issue.

You could also try taking an alternate route to work or communicating with someone in another way. Ask somebody about an area of interest and follow through on where you are led, whether it's to a book or to a seminar. It need not be something you have to do every day. The goal is to escape old, familiar patterns if they are not leading you to happiness. You can grow and learn and have fun. If you always respond to the children the same way when they come home from school, consider something totally off the wall. Consider wearing a costume and see the fun you might experience when the kids come home. The things you try can be silly. All you need to do is be different.

If you've been reluctant to let co-workers know how you feel, resolve to tell them how much you admire the way they handle themselves and how much you appreciate them. See the response you get within yourself and from these people. If you and your loved one have the same form of communicating, try leaving a note by the nightstand in the morning. Tell her you love her. Perhaps you could leave a rose. You'll be surprised at what this elicits, not only in the other person but also in you. It could bring more joy, spontaneity, creativity, and excitement to your life.

If you're used to listening to a certain type of music on your way to work or at home, buy something totally unusual. I started doing this with classical music. I found that it is soothing and wonderful to hear, so I now listen to a great deal of this music. These changes can be small at first. You might try sleeping on the other side of the bed because you're so used to one side. If you're always eating fast foods or fried foods, change your diet for a while and see what happens to your body, your coloring, and your spirit. A lot of us crave dairy products like cheese and ice cream, though we haven't been tested for the health effects. In many cases, these products can harm the functioning of our organs.

Experiment with one idea and see how it helps you. Take one step at a time. Have fun with the process. This isn't about being serious and downcast. Look at situations to discover what you can learn from them in a fun and exciting way.

The Road to Self

To accept something different in your life, you have to let go of something already in it. In letting go, confusion and fear arise, but once you go through that stage, you will find that the other side is well worth the discomfort. I experienced this on my trip. I left the familiar and endured a period of time that was totally unfamiliar. I was scared, but I had no choice but to keep going even though I was tempted to turn back. As I neared my destination, I experienced clarity, lightness, a feeling of being able to soar. I am glad I didn't retreat and run back to the familiar. I'm glad I kept pushing on to what's unknown but also exciting and alive.

There's no need to be afraid. You are not alone in pursuing change. Trust in God and the universe. You have people and tools to help you on the journey. Counseling, at times, has been helpful for me and so has astrology. Each month we go through energy cycles. When you see a full moon, take note of your reaction and you will see how the moon and other energies affect us. Astrology is a tool that can help us understand the energy that flows through a given period of time, whether it's as short as a day or as long as a lifetime. You can uncover interesting patterns through the proper use of astrology. Tools such as visualization and meditation are also available. Don't be afraid to ask for help. Talk to somebody who has experience with these things. Admit that you're confused and want help and guidance. We're all in this together, so learn how to ask for what you need. We must all support souls striving for growth.

CHAPTER
20

Visualize

Frequently, we depend too much on others' opinions. It's important to experience the world through your eyes without listening to your parents or your friends, without reading the newspaper and without letting yourself be distracted by what's happening around you. If each of us goes within and defines how we want to live and feel, we may become a little bit more compassionate. Crime, anger, and vicious acts may be transformed into love that is based on sharing, caring, and connecting to God. No longer will we turn our frustration and anger toward others.

I know this probably sounds idealistic, but principles and techniques such as visualization and trusting the inner voice can be used to help drug addicts for example. These methods have been used in housing projects, including one in Miami, where about a hundred families were guided in creative visualization and tapping the spirit within. This reduced crime, truancy rates, and the use of drugs.

In addition to healing the past, visualization can help us imagine a brighter future. I had the opportunity to listen to Roy Smalley, a former Minnesota Twins baseball player. He mentioned that he wanted to play in the All-Star game and envisioned himself doing it. He imagined what it felt like to be in the All-Star game, what it looked like, and what an All-Star player would say and do. As a result, he started responding as if he were an All-Star player and was going to be in the game. Sure enough, he became an All-Star and a World Series champion.

Creative visualization is a powerful tool. Part of this process is to believe that change can happen, and to realize that we have the ability to draw forth whatever it is that we want. We can use it to imagine how a situation will feel. That was the case with my firewalk. Using creative visualization can help you obtain what you want in your life.

CHAPTER

21

Discover Your Motivation

Because I wanted to expand my creativity, I signed up for a drawing class. The first night's assignment was to draw a pumpkin. While everyone else seemed to have drawn a pumpkin, I sketched a round pot with clingy vines. In my mind, I didn't feel talented, so I expected I would give up soon. However, I decided to keep trying; hoping that any talent I had might somehow surface.

I missed the second week but returned for the third week when the class was drawing a live model. I never completed more than the legs, and it took me two to three hours to get them to look like legs. But I managed something more than a stick man and felt a sense of accomplishment. I didn't create a masterpiece, but I did get from point A to point B, turning an incomprehensible drawing into a recognizable part of the body. My rewards from the experience far outweighed my fear.

Writing is another activity like this for me. I always found ways to avoid it versus sitting down and doing it. I was fortunate enough to come across an article by Natalie Goldberg in which she discusses the reasons people write. In some cases, it's to get love and approval. In others, it's for money, or the writer believes that what he or she has to say is vitally important. Goldberg says it's okay to take up writing because you think it will get you love. At least that motive gets you going, but it doesn't last. After a while, she says, you realize that no one cares that much, and you find another reason, perhaps money. You can dream on that awhile, but the bills pile up. Then you think, *Well, I'm a sensitive type. I have to express myself,* but it's better to be tough than sensitive because toughness will help you when you get rejected. Finally, you write because you like it.

I always thought it would be interesting to survey the top Fortune 100 CEOs to find out what motivates them. In many instances, we operate on our need for approval, on our need for things of which we're not fully aware. Once we sort out the reasons we do certain things, the picture becomes clearer. Then we can choose to continue operating this way or that way. However, we must realize that we don't have to do this because some subconscious urge is forcing us to act in certain ways. Life shouldn't be exclusively about either doing something all the time or simply being. I still feel a strong urge to produce, to be of service, and to constantly be doing rather than being. I hope to find a balance between doing and being and not spend tremendous amounts of time thinking about it. I would prefer simply to flow with what I am doing; like water flowing in a river.

CHAPTER

22

Listen to Your Gut Feeling

I had dinner with a wonderful friend who lives in Carmel and we discussed the use of intuition and psychic abilities. We talked about the times when intuition had been there for us, but we chose not to heed it and traveled down paths we wished we hadn't taken. Ultimately, we decided they were valuable experiences because we learned that intuition is a wonderful ability and we decided to trust it the next time.

He told me that a Japanese farmer had offered to buy a vineyard that he and a partner owned. His partner was out of the country, so he signed the deal. He sold the property for $700,000. This was a considerable amount of money, and he thought he had made a wise decision. His partner returned, and even though he had expressed an interest in selling the property, he had changed his mind and didn't want to go through with the sale. My friend's gut reaction was to stick with the sale, but he allowed himself to be influenced by his partner. So they hired an expensive attorney and settled with the Japanese man. They gave him $150,000 and had to pay their attorneys the same amount. So now they had their land back, but it cost them $300,000. Subsequently, the value of the land decreased to $400,000.

I told him that, although this mistake seemed costly, he had learned to listen to his intuition and perhaps now could recoup the money in other ways. It's important for us all to follow our gut instincts even when we can't pinpoint why.

Windward Pointe was a twenty-three-unit apartment complex in Florida originally financed by a bank. The developer left the project before it was finished. The bank, which had more than $2 million invested in the complex, asked if we'd consider managing the project or buying it. We worked out a deal to manage it and become a partner. We also agreed to split the proceeds if the project was converted to condominiums. Later, although the condominium market had gone soft, the bank decided to convert the project anyway.

Then, right before we were to transfer the deed, the Resolution Trust Corporation took over the bank, and they offered to sell me the project for $1,150,000. I knew that people wanted to buy the future condo units and that there was a profit of $300,000 to $400,000 to be made. However, there was a nagging feeling inside my gut.

On the surface, it seemed that everything would work and there was a profit to be made. In fact, someone offered to pay us $100,000 just for our position, which we declined. Eventually, though, the bad feelings became too much. I called the bank and said they could go ahead and convert the project to condos on their own. The bank would retain all the profits and wouldn't have to share with anybody, which they did at a healthy profit.

Some of the people involved questioned my rationale. Yet for some reason, I had a feeling deep down that, if I had done this deal, something would have happened to put us in economic difficulty. As it was, our bank told me we were at our borrowing limit and that they would have to examine the collateralization of all my loans. That was just one reason, but I am sure there were others because I was fighting the feelings constantly. Finally I said, "Okay, God, help me know what I really feel about this," and the clear answer was that I should not go ahead.

In these situations, we often spend too much time in our heads trying to figure out solutions instead of listening to our gut. So if it looks like you are forgoing a tremendous opportunity, trust your instincts and know that the reasons for your decision will become evident at some future time if you are supposed to know. In the case of this Florida project, maybe there was a bigger or better opportunity waiting around the corner. Had I done the deal, my credit lines would have been stretched and I wouldn't have been able to do anything else for at least six months. Knowing that, I'm glad I passed up the opportunity.

CHAPTER
23

Bring Your Beliefs to Work

In 1990, our company was in a period of transition. In fact, we were going to spend two days in a planning session to see where we were. I had mixed emotions about this. Planning represents an attempt to control. By trying to figure out all our next moves, we could be limiting our options. This session would be the first time in our history that we sequestered ourselves to plan our company's growth. On one hand, I hoped that our company could be fluid in response to opportunities and not limit ourselves. On the other hand, I knew by taking the time to plan, I could base my business goals on solid principles. My business philosophy is to take a long-term view of the world, come from a standpoint of high quality and integrity, and not act out of expediency.

In 1991, we opened Sidney's Pizza Cafe, a new restaurant concept that brought our quality conscious/value-oriented business philosophy to life. We offered an eclectic menu, made from scratch, cooked to order, with healthy choices served in a smoke-free environment. Sidney's became a local favorite and we were voted "Restaurateur of the Year" in 1995 by *Minneapolis/St. Paul Magazine*. We operated nine locations for over a decade, but chose to sell the restaurants to concentrate our efforts on our core business, senior living communities. However, we expanded our philosophy of providing healthy, farm-to-table, gluten-free food in a smoke-free environment to our senior living and healthcare communities.

In our real estate deals, we've never taken large developer's fees, and we always put in money just as our partners do. It gives them a sense of satisfaction to know that we're partners in these investments and that we have just as much, if not more, to lose. We believe a project is headed for success if all the money finds its way into the development rather than being used to pay fees to us and to others. Also, by taking the money available and using it to develop a product for our customers, we're able to build a substantially better project and offer it at or below market rates.

Like other industries, real estate has had major ups and downs. However, whatever your business, you will survive in the long run if you maintain integrity, offer quality and value, and examine how your philosophies affect all stakeholders including clients, customers, staff, partners, and others.

Many companies feel under pressure to consistently report higher earnings every quarter because that's how the public measures the company's success. I believe we shouldn't focus solely on economic results and ignore the process.

We should be looking at the process as something that evolves and supports the goal. Companies that take a longer view and do things appropriately with respect to their industries, their people, and the environment, see their employees as valuable resources and as partners. They look at customers' needs and value their input. Those types of companies will survive economic downturns and will flourish. I'm convinced more than ever that our business beliefs are on the right path.

In 2015, with fifty years in business, our company has over 4,000 employees and our services continue to excel. In 2014, five of the senior living and healthcare communities managed by The Goodman Group received the highest five-star rating in *U.S. News & World Report*'s "Best Nursing Homes." In 2015, The Peaks in Flagstaff, Arizona was also ranked number one for the Best Alzheimer's Care Center in the state by *Ranking Arizona* for the second consecutive year. The Goodman Group proudly received the Performance Excellence Award-Advancement level in accordance with the national Malcolm Baldrige Criteria for Performance Excellence.

To ensure our culture of service excellence, we developed Platinum Service®, an overall operating philosophy that promises to provide experiences that make people feel special. Platinum Service is exemplified by the motto: Putting you at the heart of everything we do™. Our business model is designed to be sustainable long after I am gone (or any single individual is gone).

CHAPTER
24

Show Your Vulnerability

While in Carmel, California, I had promised a group that I would go on a retreat. They were all couples and I was single, but that didn't seem to matter. However, the idea of going up to the wine country to do wine tasting and a lot of gourmet eating didn't excite me because I was not drinking alcohol or eating rich foods. I was on a fairly simple diet based on the Pritikin model. I thought, *why do this? Why not just stay in Carmel and do my exercises, and write, paint, and just be?*

I went anyway, at first out of obligation, and for the first day or two I thought, *Boy, I'm always doing things against my will to satisfy other people.* Yet as the weekend progressed, I found myself enjoying the experience. When I dismissed the notion that I was there against my will and stopped getting down on myself, I started having a good time.

For our square dance activity, we broke up into groups of four couples and learned all kinds of new terms such as corner and right-hand star. One that I already knew was do-si-do. There was also acey-deucy. I laughed so hard I almost cried. I found myself thinking that it was okay to let go of preconceived notions and to try new things. This was an experience that I will always treasure because we were like children at play. We started off as couples, but at one point, three men ended up together. The women laughed because our group tended to turn right when it should have turned left and went backward when it should have gone forward. The whole thing was pretty hysterical. It turned out to be a wonderful evening. I learned that we have to open ourselves up to new experiences because many times there'll be pleasant outcomes.

Later that weekend, a woman shared her story with me. She told me about her father, who had left the family when she was two years old. He never spent time with her or her siblings as they grew up. Just recently, she saw him at a relative's funeral, but he didn't recognize her. She cried throughout the ceremony, not only for the loss of the relative but also for the loss of the father she never knew.

As she opened up to me, we made an incredible, heartfelt connection. Then she did what most people do, myself included: She turned off her feelings. When she began to get teary-eyed again, she said that everything was okay. She suppressed her emotions. I hope that she can access them someday, but at that moment she would offer no more than she'd already shared.

It can be beautiful to share emotions. Feeling the emotion of someone's story can trigger the same emotion in the listener, who may recall similar circumstances from childhood. This can create great empathy and healing.

I enjoyed visiting with this woman. As the day continued, we talked about how men can take risks in business, but not necessarily in their personal lives. She wondered why. She then made an observation that I will always remember: She said that when a woman meets a man, she's attracted to him not because of how many business deals he can do, but because of his vulnerability and ability to be open about his emotions.

Many times illness forces people to change their lifestyles, their diets, their spiritual thinking and more. It's interesting that a lot of men I know became more emotional after having a heart attack. My wonderful friend, Zola, would cry and say, "Ever since my heart attack, I'm crying all the time," and he would get down on himself for being that way because he (like so many men) was taught to avoid displays of emotion. Yet he had such grace, lovingness and tenderness. Whenever possible, my son and I spent time with Zola before he passed on. In his frailty, in his vulnerability, he shone because he was sharing his emotions. At that time, he was so much more present to others and to himself. Maybe the heart attack opened him up to feel emotions, to feel empowered, and to realize that it's okay to cry.

It takes time and energy to suppress feelings, to lock them away, and build walls between ourselves and others. Maybe we don't want to be hurt, or to feel that we're out of control, or to show our vulnerable side. But consider the times you have been with someone who said, "You know, I didn't do it right. I messed up. I don't feel right. Something isn't right." When people show their humanity, their vulnerability, we draw closer to them because, by the grace of God, we have all been there at some time in our lives. We all experience frailty, vulnerability, and unknowingness at times.

In the coming years, I hope that our culture will open up to that childlike innocence within, allowing us to become more vulnerable, to admit that we may not have all the answers or that we are feeling a certain way. When we open up in this way, I hope that we will be listened to, supported, and accepted.

CHAPTER

25

Treasure the Gift of Time

At one time, a friend told me she felt lonely and complained that her consulting business was slow. She was used to getting up every morning and having a repetitive regimen day after day. She also thought that this was burning her out physically and emotionally. Now that she wasn't busy and had less structured time, she found herself drifting into an unfamiliar, uncomfortable new state. She was finding different issues to be concerned about, such as finances, when she should travel, what she should do, or where she should live next.

We don't usually give ourselves unstructured time. We usually want to stay active, so we set up business appointments or make social plans. If we are continually active and busy, we don't have time for thoughts of loneliness or feelings of inadequacy.

Whenever I had spare time, I made calls. I was trying to keep busy so I wouldn't have to be with myself and feel the emotions that I knew were there.

Frequently, unstructured time gets worried away and, before long, something happens to return us to our structured routine. One day, I had three hours before my next appointment and, normally, I would have kept myself busy by being on the phone talking to people. Instead, I decided to take a walk in nature and be with my body, thoughts, and emotions. Looking over the vista in Carmel Valley, I saw eight hot-air balloons rising above the morning clouds. I smelled a wood fire burning and flowers in bloom, and I realized that unstructured time is about being. It's not about worrying what we're going to do next or what we didn't do before. It's about getting out and just being present.

For years I sat around when I had some time and said to myself, I wish I were more creative. I wish I could paint or write. I wish I had a hobby. I wish I had something other than work. I would worry about this during the unstructured time and then go back to work. My discussion with my friend showed me that we should take time to be with our bodies, minds, and spirits and to experience that divinity within us.

God shows himself to us in those unstructured times, those dreamlike states, and those times of just being. I've had my greatest breakthroughs in that downtime, that quiet time. When our minds are busy with chatter, we don't allow energies to flow through us and we don't listen to our inner voice. I've found that being in the woods or around water allows me to be receptive. In those settings I become more in tune with nature's guidance and with the universal energy that flows through nature. Each person knows best where he can be open and tune in to these energies. You can experience an "aha" moment that ends up having the most profound effect on your life.

Here is an interesting experiment: stop scheduling everything and see what happens. Now, many people will cite responsibilities to employers, children, or community activities as to why this is impossible. However, this isn't about changing your whole life overnight. This is about experimenting.

Leave time open and see what you do with it. With a new day can come a new feeling of excitement and exuberance if you believe it. See what it's like to start your day without preconceived ideas about what you have to accomplish. As something comes to mind or you experience a feeling, act on it. This exercise is not about inactivity. The goal is to recognize that you don't know all the answers and don't need to control everything at every moment.

You must leave room for the magical and mystical universe to help support you in your daily regimen. Once you've experimented with this concept, you'll realize that it could work in all areas of your life. You might realize a job change or living someplace else is possible. Instead of trying to figure it all out, leave the question open and say, "Okay, universe, if I am supposed to make a change, give me a signal, a reason, an understanding, a feeling that helps move me in the direction that I need to take."

CHAPTER
26

Empower Yourself

To get the most out of life, we must trust ourselves and our connectedness to divine energy. If we can learn how to trust and get in touch with that spirituality, we can become in tune with the universe and with the natural flow of energies. Then we can start making decisions from that power source within us. We can learn how to take back our own power, to be strong in our convictions, not to be swayed by others, and to know that our inner knowledge rings true and is there to guide and to support us.

Observe in your daily inner psyche when others are coming from that true centeredness. When they are in tune with this energy, you will find their facial and tonal qualities and body postures are totally different than if they were wrestling with an issue. I'm sure there have been times when you've known something right down to your core. We have all the answers we'll ever need within us, and our responsibility is to learn how to access those answers. Unfortunately, we think that we have to control everything and that we have to be the one to push all the buttons instead of trusting that the universe will give us whatever we need when we need it.

Start using these concepts to see how strong you are and how you can stop becoming a victim of other people's whims and desires. Then you will be in control of what you think and how you feel rather than allowing a parent, a spouse, a boss, or a fellow employee to determine your thinking. The more you practice this, the more you will realize your own power and take it back. The stronger you get, the more decisive you will become in your daily activities. You will come from a place of empowerment, and you won't have to look back and worry about the consequences. You will make decisions and move on to something else, decreasing the time spent wrestling with problems in your mind.

Tony Robbins has an interesting exercise that you might want to try. Draw an imaginary circle in front of you and while you're outside the circle, view it as a place of empowerment. Then imagine how you'd feel if you were totally empowered. How would you breathe? What would your posture be, and what would you be doing with your hands? You might be standing upright, with your chest out and your head up. Feel how that might be and view it. When you have that scene in your mind, step inside the circle and feel what it's like to be empowered and what it's like to come from that point of knowingness, that point of assurance. After you've experienced that, step outside the circle and see what happens to your physiology, to your breathing. You can access that feeling any time you desire. It's about belief, being connected, and knowing something right down to your very core. That essence comes with us and follows us through this lifetime and many lifetimes.

As children, we're aware of that inner knowingness, but life's events interject themselves. We start to experience self-doubt, and with self-doubt comes self-criticism. Our self-esteem decreases, and we start disbelieving in our power source and questioning our ability to make decisions. Then we spend much more time in our heads than with that power source.

We must reclaim the power that each of us was given at birth, the power that we carry with us from life to life. It's always with us, and all we have to do is look inside and accept it. The more we do this, the more we'll realize that we can write our own script in every situation. We no longer have to fall prey to what people have told us about how life has to be hard or how we're not able to achieve abundance. We can become our own architects. We can become our own scriptwriters. Each one of us has that ability. All we have to do is give ourselves permission to use it.

CHAPTER
27

Heal Your Fear,
Heal Your Anger

My father and I had a major disagreement over a restaurant we had opened in Billings, Montana. He wanted to have gambling machines and serve liquor. But it was a family restaurant, and I didn't want gambling. Our discussion became so heated that he said he was going to get an attorney to separate his things from mine. At that moment, I was prepared to let go of everything for the sake of happiness and was not attached to the material possessions, the office, or the business. I was ready to let the company go. I was no longer angry with my father, but I realized the disagreement had been necessary for some inexplicable reason. This was not the first time that he had threatened to dismantle the partnership we'd spent years putting together. I was tired of the threats. I didn't like the feeling of confrontation and wanted to call my father and tell him so.

Fortunately, a couple of things happened. My father returned and we talked. He was very concerned about me and the fact that I had gotten so angry when he thought he was just being helpful. I told him what was happening in my life and how issues from my childhood were returning. I told him that I felt healthier, but to get healthy and stay that way, I had to express emotions stored inside me for years. We talked, both of us crying at times, and said we cared about each other and loved each other and didn't want to separate. I told Dad that I needed him to hang in there and support me while I worked through my problems and that I would succeed.

The second fortunate event that day was my visit to a chiropractor. I mentioned my issue with my father, and the doctor recommended a homeopathic remedy called "Gaillardia." This Texas wildflower enhances the determination to succeed despite obstacles. Gaillardia lightens the stubborn personality with the joy of overcoming. This effect is associated with the oldest part of the immune system, macrophage activity. When these dinosaurs of the immune system move into action, nothing can stop them. They can change shapes, squeeze through tissues and inner cellular spaces, and engulf foreign or damaged cells. Macrophages disintegrate their foes by showering them with strong enzymes and hydrogen peroxide made within the body. Gaillardia promotes our latent ability to overcome opposition and difficulties no matter what obstacles confront us.

However, my anger required more than Gaillardia or sitting and meditating and hoping that the energy would dispel itself. Every time I thought about the issues with my father, it triggered my rage. I needed to go into the woods to exercise and vent my anger by screaming and, if necessary, throwing rocks and even chopping down trees. In addition to physical activity in the outdoors, I realized that I needed muscle and deep tissue work.

To release the anger and rage stored inside me, I embarked upon a hike into the woods. I wanted to learn how to let these feelings come out in a safe and healthy way rather than affecting those around me. I prayed that God would help me get in touch with these emotions and release them in a way that wasn't destructive to me. The last time I tried this during some family counseling, I was jumping up and down and hitting a pillow and my back went out. I think that was when I herniated a disc. I have long thought that when we release anger, something destructive happens to others or to us.

I went to a hardware store to shop for an ax so that I could chop dead wood and dispel some of my frustration. Remembering the family counseling injury, I thought I would be smart. I bought an ax, but as a precaution I also bought an extra ax handle with no blade because I didn't want to lose an appendage. As I drove toward Garland State Park in Carmel, my courage increased, and when I got there I decided to take the ax and not the extra ax handle. I wanted to ask a ranger if it was okay to chop wood that had already fallen and started to decay, but nobody was around, so I started on my trek. I walked up the side of a hill, saw some dead wood and took a couple of swipes at it. The first one almost hit my foot. I thought, *Oh no, I should have gone for a walk or stayed in the car.*

Then I thought, *Just wait a minute. Center and stay focused on what you are trying to do.* I started again, but now I worried that maybe I was doing something wrong and shouldn't be chopping dead wood and that somebody would come along and tell me to quit. So I stopped again and cleared my mind. I said, "Give yourself permission, John, to express your anger. Let it flow." Then it was like a dam burst and things from way back were being released. I got the anger to the surface and chopped wood almost to the point of exhaustion.

When I was done, probably about fifteen or twenty minutes later, I knew that something had happened. I didn't know exactly what, but that wasn't important. It seemed like some of the tension had dissipated. I put my ax back in my backpack and continued on my journey through Garland Park. It was a wonderful experience. I felt freer. Usually when you experience anger and rage, you find another underlying emotion that must be worked out.

I've learned we shouldn't sit in judgment of one another because we've all made mistakes; we've all done things we have been sorry for; we've all hurt people and wished we hadn't. In being kind to yourself, you also need to be kind and forgiving to others. Unspoken resentment, anger, and hostility toward other human beings can cause physical and emotional problems for the one harboring these feelings. We must not suppress these emotions but allow ourselves to feel them and let them go.

This doesn't necessarily mean confrontation. There are plenty of ways to deal with frustration, anger, and hurt. The key is to understand those feelings and look at the people and situations causing them in a forgiving and healing way. As you do that, you will be surprised to see how the energy changes. If you are separated from a person by long distance, once the process is completed you might hear from him through a letter or a phone call, or you might run into him and discover all those past hurts have vanished. Even if that person has passed away, visualize the person surrounded by white light and tell him or her what you want to say. If we're all energy and we're all linked in some way, our energies will connect.

CHAPTER

28

Release and Receive

I told my therapist that I thought my father and I should do counseling together. I made an appointment with her and fortunately my father said he would accompany me. It was a fascinating experience. Our session with the counselor was the first time that I'd heard my father say what caused him to act and react as he did when I was younger. At that age, I didn't know what was going on with my family. It was enlightening to hear my father speak about his feelings of inadequacy when he was young and how he tried to parent to the best of his ability. I was in tears listening to my father tell me about the love he always had for me and how proud he was of me. I felt such gratitude that we were able to sit together and not get defensive, to forgive one another, and to love each other. I believe that if my father had been dead, I could have resolved this issue by forgiving him, but I was fortunate to have him there to work through this together.

When you confront your issues from the past, try to come from a loving place of communication, forgiveness, and empathy. Get the emotional part out so it isn't released in frustration and rage, resulting in more anger. The goal isn't to get someone else to change. We need to share our emotions to let the love come forward and be shared. Sometimes this feels uncomfortable because it's strange territory. I know that it was strange for my father. On the lighter side, Dad had never gotten a massage. There is a wonderful place in Big Sur called Esalen and I wanted to share this beautiful setting with him. I made noon appointments for us to get massages on the deck. I could see my father's resistance the next day as we drove there. At about 11:30 a.m. he said, "I'm hungry. Let's stop for lunch." I told him we had to get to our appointments. He told me he wasn't going to be pushed, so I finally pulled into a grocery store, ordered him a sandwich and soup, and we had lunch on the curb.

Fortunately, we got to our massage appointments just at noon and my father had this terrific woman give him a massage. He asked her about everything that had happened in her life, but eventually he settled down. I was finished before he was and I saw him lying on the table, looking rested. She was singing a song to him, and at that moment I realized we are all souls linked to each other and we are all vulnerable and childlike. It was a unique moment to see my father not helpless but at peace, just being and receiving, something I had seen so infrequently. I always saw him as the one giving, and it moved me to see him receiving, being still, and taking in the energy around him.

When he was done, he felt wonderful. He said, "This is what I've been missing." Once again, I realized that "when we always do what we've always done, we always get what we've always gotten." In opening up and allowing change to come into his life, Dad was learning the possibilities of being nurtured and accepting help rather than always being the one who has to give.

CHAPTER

29

See Life from the Inside Out

I woke up one morning and the upper eyelid of my left eye was puffed up. I had gotten some type of infection but I didn't do much about it. My father told me to soak the eye and see a doctor if it didn't get better. I let it go and got more sties on my lower eyelids. Finally, after a couple of weeks, I went to a doctor and he wanted to cut them open. Instead I saw another doctor and got a prescription. I filled the prescription but didn't use it. I thought that maybe the discharge from the sties was part of a healing process.

After about three weeks, I saw my therapist and she asked me in our guided imagery how I was feeling. I told her I had tremendous peace and gratitude for the healing I had experienced with my father and for getting through my anger. I told her of the gratitude and joy I felt at being alive. I said some emotional issue might have arisen, because I was having problems with my eyes, but I didn't know of anything because I felt joyous. She told me to lie down and to go within. In my meditation, it came to me that I was to put a cold compress on my eyes. She got a cold washcloth and I put it on my eyes, and suddenly things started happening.

First, I realized that I'd been seeing my life from the outside in and that I needed to see the world from the inside out. For the next two to three weeks, I regularly put a cold compress over my eyes. Each time I used the compress, I felt a light within me. This light had cones, almost like rods, emanating from it. They were bright and full of energy, and I felt like my whole body had been electrified. It was an incredibly warm and nurturing feeling!

I finally got what was happening. The problem with my eyes was helping me to go within and develop a spiritual connection with God. The next day my eyes stopped itching and started to heal. It was amazing. My body was changing its composition. As the anger and rage dissipated and my spiritual awakening occurred, toxins and metals stored in my body were released and adhesions that were so bound up in my muscles were diminishing.

The process of healing the wounded child within occurs on emotional, physical, and spiritual levels. Even though it sometimes seems to be a long and arduous process, it is well worth the effort. I believe that, in time, there will be more places where we can have our physical, spiritual, mental, and emotional needs assessed and it will be more accepted that we can heal from the inside out. Also, as we heal ourselves, we can be conduits to help heal others.

CHAPTER
30

Expect Miracles

In November 1990, The Goodman Group invited authors Dr. Jerry Jampolsky and Dr. Diane Cirincione-Jampolsky to speak to the residents and staff of the Palms of Largo, one of our senior living communities. We planned to head down to Longboat Key the next day where Jerry and Diane would open our company planning session. Then our staff, my father, and I would explore where we were as a company and where we wanted to be over the next few years.

The night before they were to speak to the residents, Jerry, Diane, the corporate office staff, and I went to dinner. I found myself feeling listless and tense. The next morning, I woke up feeling frustrated and angry. I didn't know how we'd accomplish everything we needed to do to further my vision for senior housing. Given all the details and time, I was starting to think turning this vision into reality was impossible. I wasn't sure that anything I was doing would make a difference, and I thought maybe I should stop caring and just move forward.

Around noon I picked up Jerry and Diane, and I shared with Jerry my frustration about the details of my vision. I had lost my centeredness and my trust that the universe would fill in the blanks. Jerry told me that when he had been a psychiatrist earlier in life, if he had a speaking engagement, he would write his speech beforehand so that he knew exactly what he was going to say. Then he met an older woman who told him, "You won't have a believable speech until you get up and speak from your heart." She told him if he didn't have it so figured out ahead of time, he'd become more believable. So I decided I wouldn't prepare any remarks and I would get up and let the universal energies flow through me, confident that I would say what I needed to say.

When we reached the parking lot, the miracles began unfolding. We got out of the car and Jerry said, "Let's stop for a moment and say a prayer." There we were, holding hands behind the car as people walked by, our heads bowed and eyes closed for a few moments of wonderful silence and prayer. The energy was flowing. When I entered the building, I had a desire to sit and be alone with God and ask him for guidance. I looked for a private place, but there were people all around, so I retreated to the men's bathroom. I sat on a toilet seat and asked God for help and guidance.

After being introduced, I got up and spoke to a group of about 450 residents and staff. When I opened my mouth, God took over. I shared with everyone that I had just been meditating on the toilet seat. We all laughed and immediately I had a connection with everyone. They knew I was speaking from the heart. I also discussed the creation of Palms of Largo and said our intent in building the senior living residence was not only to create a beautiful community but also to instill life in it. We wanted people to learn, and we hoped to offer them a more joyful existence by providing programs that would help them grow in body, mind, spirit, and emotion.

We then showed an eight-minute video on the Palms of Largo. I sat down, and that's when another miracle happened. The film jiggled on the screen. Evidently the vertical hold couldn't be adjusted, and I found myself getting angrier and angrier at the constant flickering. But then I saw the beauty of what was happening, and I realized I could get caught up in the details or I could be in the moment and trust that everything would be okay. I chose to do the latter, and suddenly the energy in me changed and I started listening to the words and wasn't so focused on the mechanics. I heard what was being said, and I identified with it. I learned that even if things weren't perfect, everything was okay. Because we are human, we will make mistakes. I realized that if we search for perfection, which supposedly will make us happy, we would never be happy because there is no such thing as perfection.

After the video finished, I introduced Jerry and Diane and they spoke for the better part of two hours. They talked about Jerry's mother Tilly, who spent a great deal of time contradicting Jerry's belief system. In fact, he wrote so many books on forgiveness that one day she told him she was going to write a book on unforgiveness!

Eventually, Jerry and Diane realized their interactions with Tilly were essentially a script. Whatever they did wasn't good enough. Whenever they visited her, they weren't there long enough. If they were there two hours, she would expect them to spend five hours, and if they were there one hour, she would expect them to spend three hours. They also realized they had roles and lines too. They were always trying to change her.

Finally, one day, they decided they were going to change the script. They would let go of their expectations and accept Tilly for who she is. To their amazement, when they let go of changing her, a real change took place! Tilly became interested in what they were doing. On one visit, Jerry and Diane had to leave shortly after they got there, and his mother said, "If you have to go, I don't want to keep you." Jerry's mouth dropped open. When they changed their expectations, the change in his mother automatically took place.

That's a lesson for many of us. If we stop pursuing an outcome and let go of our expectations, then we automatically free ourselves from a negative space. It's no longer possible for somebody else to push our buttons by refusing to give us what we want.

Jerry and Diane also talked about a seventeen-year-old girl who had a terminal illness. They asked her if she had one last wish, what it would be. She said she would like to heal all the relationships in which she had hurt someone or someone had hurt her. Prior to her passing, she mentioned she had healed those relationships. Jerry and Diane said when she died there was an air of absolute calmness and peace over her.

When we hang on to our anger and insist on our righteousness, we lock that energy inside us and it can't flow freely. Sometimes we don't want to heal relationships because we think that would make the other person right and us wrong. We become used to not forgiving. But forgiveness is worthwhile for our own peace of mind. Forgiving people who have hurt us also means we are forgiving ourselves. We must unlock that negative energy within and allow ourselves to be free flowing. The desire to live more joyfully is reason enough to be forgiving of others.

Jerry and Diane also discussed perception and the adage about whether the glass is half empty or half full. We may not be able to change the past, but we can change our perceptions of it and of current situations. How we view the world and live is our choice. They said we must choose love because anything other than love is fear. Anger, rage, and jealousy all fall under the fear category, and while we're in a place of fear, it's difficult to experience love.

During the lecture, another miracle took place. There were two lights over the stage, and one light kept flickering every two minutes throughout the two-hour talk. Every time it happened, I would look up and say to myself, "Okay, do you want to become angry because something isn't working properly, or do you want to sit and listen?" I was not in control. Just like when the video was flickering, I knew that I couldn't affect those lights. I couldn't turn them on or off. So, after they had flickered for about the fifth time, I decided to ignore the situation. As it turned out, the problem didn't affect the taping and it certainly didn't affect the group because when Jerry and Diane finished they received a standing ovation.

The energy in the room was amazing. Everybody felt a sharing, a complete oneness. Our differences vanished, and we seemed to be connected to a higher being and an energy that supported and protected us. It was a miracle to have heard Jerry and Diane's lecture. Many people came up to me and said they experienced a tremendous freeing and a change within. One of our administrators hugged me and said, "Don't say anything because if you do, I'm just going to break into tears." She was visibly moved. Later, while she was talking with Jerry and Diane, her tears flowed as she experienced a wonderful catharsis.

I had started the day concerned about who would help with the details of my vision and how it would get done. Ten minutes after Jerry and Diane finished speaking, several people came up to me and offered their services. I had mentioned that we were looking for somebody to set up *A Course in Miracles* program with a daily reading on spirituality and fellowship. This was also a program that had inspired Jerry. A man and his wife approached me after the lecture. He had just retired, and for the past thirteen years he had helped create study groups for a fellowship course. He volunteered to help with our project. I looked up over his shoulder and said, "Thank you, God."

The next person to approach me was a woman who said, "I once had cancer and was able to cure my cancer, and a lot of it had to do with laughter and with improvisational theater; in fact, I've become a stand-up comic, and I've been thinking of ways to help others in gratitude for my healing. I'd like to help the people in your community and set up classes on laughter and improv." Next a man gave me his card, which said, "Listener." I had heard Jerry and Diane speak about our ability to listen. What a loving and healing way to support people. I asked the man if he would consider setting up a class on listening and teach us to become better listeners. His eyes lit up and he said he would be glad to do that.

We planned to launch the Sage College at the Palms of Largo to offer classes on body, mind, spirit, and emotion. Residents could be teachers as well as students, and the college would be open to the community at large. We distributed the flyer inviting community participation. I was amazed. That morning, I had felt overwhelmed, wondering how to accomplish everything. Then that afternoon, in a period of ten minutes, three lovely people had offered their services to help start classes at the college.

Then a fourth person appeared. Marilyn, who for many years had known Jerry and Diane and had worked at the Center of Attitudinal Healing in Tiburon, California, had tremendous experience in creating programming and setting up support groups. We were looking for an overall program coordinator at the Palms of Largo. Marilyn joined our staff meeting and listened. Unbeknownst to me, Jerry and Diane had invited her to the Royal Palms residence for dinner. I sat with her after the meeting, and before the day was over, I had invited her to our staff retreat, knowing within that she would probably assist us in setting up our body, mind, spirit, and emotion programming. That was another miracle, and the day kept unfolding with them. In my moment of despair, I had turned the matter over to God and asked for help and guidance, and when I opened up to that guidance, it flowed all day and night.

Not everything was roses. On the way home that night, Jerry and Diane candidly talked to me about my management practices. I'd been sending mixed messages. I told people that I wanted them to be independent, make their own decisions, and use their own judgment. Frequently, though, I looked over their shoulder and was quick to criticize if something wasn't done the way I thought it should be. People weren't truly empowered and didn't feel free to communicate.

They asked how we wanted to run the company. Did we want vertical management, with one person on top and other people carrying out the leader's wishes? Or did we want a lateral type of organization that requires open communication among all levels? Truthfully, I wanted some of both. I realized that my management style didn't have to be perfect, but I should be trying to find a situation where everybody could win.

For most of my first twenty years of working, I felt I had to be everything to everybody. I had to be the visionary, and the one who made sure that plans were implemented. I had a lot of people in my organization who were wonderful at carrying out plans, but I'm not sure if they felt free to express their feelings and opinions. They probably feared they'd be perceived as creating disharmony. I realized I needed to establish consistent and concise communication lines among staff members and get them what they needed to accomplish company goals.

When Jerry and Diane returned to Royal Palms for dinner, a Southern Baptist minister who had heard the lecture asked Jerry to talk with him. Their interaction was interesting. The minister said he agreed with Jerry, but Jerry was missing the essence: an acknowledgment of Jesus and a continual response to him. Listening to this dialogue was a blessing. The minister had clearly put the lecture through his own filter system.

Implicit in Jerry and Diane's discussion was the acknowledgment of a higher power within us. This is our connection to the divine. Whether you call it God, Jesus, or some other name, it's a source available to all. I can see sometimes how religion can be at loggerheads with spirituality. Though spirituality exists in all of us, religion is formatted and delivered in a certain way. I felt fortunate to observe this interaction because I realized that unless we can acknowledge our oneness and our sameness and the universal energy that flows through all of us, we will get caught up in dogma and keep playing mental chess games to prove our points. I hope that while people retain whatever dogma or mental imagery is necessary for them, they can also accept the spirituality that permeates and unites us all.

Without a doubt, it was a day of miracles. I will always remember being open to divine intervention, which allowed the miracles to happen. All we need to do is be open and ask God for guidance and for help.

CHAPTER

31

Be the Change

The next day, Jerry, Diane, my father, and I traveled by boat from Clearwater to Longboat Key to meet with seven members of the team. We were hosting a retreat to determine where we were as a company and where we were headed. The forty-mile trip took a little more than three hours.

Everything was functioning pretty smoothly on the boat ride until I saw a red light marker. It wasn't a regular channel marker, so I had to make a quick decision about which side to pass on. The right side seemed to be the appropriate one, so I slowed down for a look, which was fortunate because it wasn't too long before the boat ran out of water and we were stuck on mudflats. We were able to dig a new channel with our props, and after about forty-five minutes, we freed ourselves by going backward and forward, much like getting a car out of a snow rut.

During this time, I observed everybody's reactions. Jerry sat relaxed in the back of the boat; his facial expression never changed. He chose to remain calm. My father chose to pace. I thought I was pretty calm but found that I was sweating profusely. I thought Jerry's calmness in a fairly tense situation was admirable. He was peaceful before, and he had chosen to remain peaceful during and after the incident.

Once freed, we continued to Longboat Key. We intended to go down earlier so Jerry and Diane could help set the stage for our retreat before they had to leave. I now realize the universe had put a roadblock in our way because the group was supposed to function by itself without outside facilitation.

I had no idea how the team session would go. We had a set agenda, but I asked that it be put aside to see what would happen. The miracles continued. Previously, I said that my primary goals for the company were quality, integrity, and honesty and that everything we do must be measured against those goals. On this day, I shared that I wanted to move forward and be constructive rather than go backward and be destructive. I explained that I wanted the ability to create rather than manage and that I wanted to be around people who "walked their talk." I asked the management team to create more effective measuring sticks to draw a line between the profit motive and the human spirit motive.

I shared that I was more interested in developing human potential than in extracting dollars. (I'm not against making money, but I believe that if quality, integrity, and honesty are observed, the bottom line will fall into place.) I also shared that I wanted to be able to express my feelings, be myself, and delegate, but that I needed support in doing so. I wanted to be more present, not in fourteen different places.

I then asked all the people in the room to share their goals, strengths, weaknesses, and feelings. They had different thoughts about how the workplace should handle emotional life. As the leader and the facilitator, I thought we should offer a supportive environment and let those who wanted to be expressive feel free to show their emotions. At the same time, we had to honor and respect those who wanted to reserve their emotions for another environment.

One manager said for years he would leave his emotions in the garage and go to work, and when he came home he would pick them up in the garage and go in the door. He wanted to lift the limitations that he placed on himself, to continue learning, and to make a contribution to the company and to his family.

He worried that work was taking time away from his wife and children and his family was taking time away from his work. So we explored the possibility of setting up an alternative workspace for him.

Another manager said that this exercise was useless but he would participate. He didn't feel comfortable sharing his emotions and didn't want to delve into this area. Concerning his goals, he wanted employees to be happy and enjoy adequate compensation. He said that when things were going well, he was being paid too much, but that when things were going badly, he wasn't being paid enough. Everybody agreed with him on that point.

Sharing helped the group to realize that some of our responses on the job stemmed from our childhood experiences. We were not totally aware of this until we had the opportunity to examine this idea. Two individuals realized that they were always trying to please people and win approval. As they spoke, they realized the pattern had been created at a young age for them because they had always tried to please their fathers.

All these people are wonderful, loving human beings and I found that I was starting to value each individual's uniqueness and inner beauty; in doing so, I saw my own inner beauty more. It was quite an experience.

We ended with my father, and this was another miracle. Dad's goals were happiness and contentment. He talked about his desire to express himself and to feel comfortable and cared for, and he wanted to know where he fit in. He wanted to make sure that we were striving to decrease the company's debt. He thought it was important to have the company stick with what it does best.

Dad, who was seventy at the time, had often said that people his age couldn't change. "I don't want to change," he would say. "I am who I am, and this is the way I've been and this is the way I'll die." When he spoke this day, he said, "You can change." I was stunned. I asked him to repeat that because I thought he'd said can't. He repeated the line and then told us about his earlier days in business.

He had sold his beer distributorship and put all the money he had into the medical building where we had our offices for many years. He thought that was always going to be his building, his future, so when I told him that we were going to sell the building, he said, "No, you're not." I said, "Yes, we are," and he shot back, "Over my dead body you're going to sell this building. I'm not going to move out of here." Eventually, as I mentioned earlier, the sale took place, and we made the move. Dad did so reluctantly and grudgingly, still thinking that we'd made a mistake. Now, for the first time, he acknowledged that although he had resisted the change, he realized it was the best thing that had ever happened to him and to the company. With that, we both started to cry. I hugged Dad and felt an incredible soul connection with him.

As Dad opened up and cried, he became aware that he was expressing his emotions and said, "Oh, that stroke that I had a few years ago is doing this to me." At that point, we thanked him for sharing his true self with us. He had brought tremendous healing to himself, to me, and to the others. My dad, who had seemed inflexible and resistant to change, was there for all of us. He had revealed his vulnerable side and showed us that change can take place. We realized that he was doing his best. After this, we talked some more and said prayers of thanks as we gathered in a circle. We hugged each other, held hands, and appreciated the wonderfulness of the day. My father showed me, and others, that change is possible at any age. We must learn how to forgive each other and to love the essence of every human being. I will always remember my dad as a wonderful teacher and a truly loving soul.

CHAPTER
32

Love Always

At forty-one years old, I felt I had never known love. I had known need and dependency and had learned karmic lessons. Sadly, I didn't believe I'd experienced the unconditional love that we all long to enjoy. I always hoped to experience it and to become at peace with the flow of the universe and with the God-like spirit within us. I realized part of that, if not all, involved love: love of self, love of others, and love of mankind. When that love is there, you attract another spirit. This kind of love is not all consuming. It maintains the separateness of souls but allows the coming together of two spirits. Two separate souls come together to produce more than they could alone. I still hope for this type of relationship.

Ultimately, love is why we're here. It is what we're here to learn, to give, and to receive. Anything other than that is fear, which gets in the way of our relationships. A lot of our power struggles come from a lack of love or perceived lack of love. We lack trust in God and feel separated from Him, from ourselves, and from one another. If we learn to love ourselves and to accept our union with God and with our fellow man, love can come freely. Then confrontations will subside and we can start living healthier, more joyful lives.

Now at age sixty-six, I realize my whole life is a road trip, an exploration, and an adventure. I've learned a lot along the way and I'm grateful. I find that love is more relevant than ever. I truly had to do the inner work on myself. I have to be it. Love it. Not just speak it.

About the Author

J ohn B. Goodman, Chairman of The Goodman Group, has spent 45 years building a family property management company into an award-winning organization that creates and manages living environments that emphasize quality of life. He attributes his success to a holistic approach, one that recognizes the whole individual; body, mind, and spirit. The Goodman Group's innovative programs bring to life quality conscious/value oriented principles, and enable residents and staff to achieve an optimum level of wellbeing.

John has been a featured speaker at the Massachusetts Institute of Technology, the National Association of Senior Living Industries, and the University of Minnesota Carlson School of Management. He is committed to providing leadership that fosters personal growth and achievement, along with creating ways in which business can play a positive role in society.

He is the recipient of the 2002 Ellis Island Medal of Honor and in 2011 was named Citizen of the Year by Florida's Largo Mid-Pinellas Chamber of Commerce. In 2015, The Goodman Group proudly received the Performance Excellence Award-Advancement level in accordance with the national Malcolm Baldrige Criteria for Performance Excellence.

To learn more about The Goodman Group visit
www.thegoodmangroup.com